*Publisher's
note*

Encyclopædia Britannica, Inc.
is proud to have played a part in the publication
of this memorial
to the late President of the United States,
whose loss so affected
his country and the entire world.
We are grateful, too, in the knowledge
that the proceeds from the sale of this book
will be given over to the support of
The John Fitzgerald Kennedy Memorial
Library, in Cambridge, Massachusetts.

Authorized by the Trustees of The John
Fitzgerald Kennedy Memorial Library

". . . .we'll never be young again."

A TRIBUTE

TO

JOHN F. KENNEDY

Edited by
Pierre Salinger
and
Sander Vanocur

ENCYCLOPAEDIA BRITANNICA, INC.

Chicago

Dedication
by
President Lyndon B. Johnson

There could have been a thousand more tributes in this book.

But this would not have been to John Kennedy's taste. He was a man of quality who, with all his disciplines, resisted the reach for mere quantity.

I knew him as my President—as my fellow legislator—but most of all, I knew him as a human being, a good man, a great man.

This book, and all that is in it, is dedicated to John Fitzgerald Kennedy who wanted so much to bring new hope to the world —and who, in a tragically brief opportunity, set our course to fulfill his dream.

T his is a book of tributes to John F. Kennedy. He wouldn't like it much. John Kennedy didn't go in for tributes.

Millions of words were written and spoken about John Kennedy after his assassination. They were heartfelt and sincere words which reflected the agony of peoples and nations. But much of what was written missed the real John F. Kennedy.

Much was written about his power and his wealth and the fact that he faced nuclear war and did not flinch.

But John Kennedy was more than a powerful man, or a wealthy man, or a man with steel nerves.

He was a gentle and compassionate man. Because he loved people he did not view the world and its problems in an abstract way. The *campesino* in Latin America, the American boy dying in Viet Nam, the small boy starving to death in an Indian village, the child born retarded, were not statistics to him. They were people, to be helped, to be loved, and not to be forgotten.

John Kennedy was blessed with a beautiful and courageous wife and two wonderful children. He loved them all, deeply and warmly. One could not see him for a minute with his children and not realize the bond of friendship and understanding and love that existed between them. But one could not see John Kennedy standing in the boiler room of a Boston hospital, tears streaming down his face, after the death of his baby son and not understand how deeply he had been hurt.

John Kennedy had warmth and humor. He admired brilliance and excellence. He tolerated honest mistakes but never stupidity. He rejected phoniness. But he could not bring himself to hurt anyone.

These pages are limited and so are the words. This book has been very hard to put together. We have not sought quantity. We have looked for the kind of tributes he might have tolerated, the warm recollections of friends, the warm reminiscences of persons whose lives he touched only briefly; the letters of little children; the words of people in foreign lands whom he never met but who somehow understood him better than some of his own countrymen.

As for me, John F. Kennedy gave me something that no one can take away—the privilege of working with him for four wonderful, turbulent years. It is to these four years—to times of happiness and sadness, to times of crisis and times of calm, to times of work and times of play—that I dedicate my part of his book. There is really no other way I can repay him now.

Pierre Salinger is right. John F. Kennedy would not like this book. But he would read it. He read everything he could lay his hands on. I know. The last time I saw him in his office was during the summer of 1963. It was a Friday afternoon and he was preparing to leave for a weekend at Hyannisport. I had put a copy of *The Economist* on a table outside his office before going in to see him. When our brief talk had ended, he walked with me to the door, picked up *The Economist* lying on the table and started flipping through its pages as he walked to the waiting helicopter. In the early days of his campaigning for the Presidency, you couldn't leave a newspaper or a magazine unguarded on his plane. If you did, he would grab it and you would never see it again.

He loved words used well and he knew their power. That is why I think he would have hated the idea of a book of tributes, but would have rejoiced in seeing how the words in this book have evoked a powerful sense of what manner of man he was and the impact he made upon his time.

A Kennedy myth is already being created. We have no desire to add to it. Myths need no help. They feed upon themselves as they grow. John F. Kennedy was no myth. He was an imperfect man who knew he had "promises to keep and miles to go" before time cheated him. What we have collected in this book was written and said under the terrible weight of an immediate loss. We prefer this tribute because it seemed such a waste for so many kind words about this man to be so soon forgotten. It is the least we can do. The years were so good, the future was so bright.

Foreword
by
Theodore C. Sorensen

On the 22nd of November 1963, three shots rang out under a Texas sky—and the brightest light of our time was snuffed out by senseless evil. The voice which had always been calm even in the face of adversity was silenced. The heart which had always been kind even in the midst of emergency was stopped. And the laugh which had always been gay even in reply to abuse was heard no more in the land.

Crowds waited all night in the cold and the wet to pass by his coffin in the dawn. They wept on the streets of Moscow. They prayed in the villages of Asia. They brought candles to the Wall in West Berlin. Elders who had scoffed at his youth felt suddenly that they had been orphaned. Youth who had been impatient with his patience felt suddenly older and greyer. And those of us who knew and served and loved him felt, as the Irish felt on the death of Owen Roe O'Neill, that we were lost and alone.

"sheep without a shepherd when the snow shuts out the sky—
O why did you leave us . . . why did you die?"

For all of us, life goes on—but brightness has fallen from the air. The world continues in the same orbit—but it is a different world. His hand-picked successor has picked up the fallen torch and carries it proudly and ably forward—but a Golden age is over and it will never be again.

For John Fitzgerald Kennedy was not an ordinary man, in either life or death. He was the first President born in this century, the first of the Catholic faith, the first to reach out to space, the first to bear throughout his term the awful and awesome obligation of the age of mutual destruction.

He was also the first, with the possible exception of Jefferson, to care so deeply about the quality of American life and its meaning in the world. There were poets and performers at his Inaugural. There were princes and prime ministers at his funeral. That special Kennedy quality that some called by the superficial name of "style" was in reality his insistence on excellence—excellence for his country and for himself, excellence in matters of talent as well as taste.

For he believed in the good society as well as the good life. He restored learning to the seats of power, politics as a profession of respect and pride in the hearts of his countrymen.

He was eloquent but never pompous, tough but always gentle, an idealist but still a realist. He knew when to reflect and when to act. He was a student of the past and a prophet of the future, a thinker and doer who both studied history and changed it. He always saw the larger picture while demanding all details. He thought of the next generation as well as his own —and he understood the difference between patience and hesitation.

President Kennedy was unique in public life. For he truly did not ask what his country could do for him—only what he could do for his country. He inspired the loyalty of his associates, yet encouraged us to dissent. Beloved by his political friends, he courted his political enemies. He took the world very seriously but he never took himself too seriously. He accepted blame that others sought to evade and he shattered precedents that others thought unbreakable.

In a world caught up in a series of peaceful and not so peaceful revolutions—revolutions for which his countrymen and Congress were not always fully prepared—he charted new

15

courses with caution as well as courage. He did not try to force solutions but to find them—and his restraint was born not out of irresolution but out of reason.

In the end he was struck down by the very malice and madness he had sought to cast out—an ironic victim of the extreme left in a citadel of the extreme right.

John Kennedy died as he would have wanted to die—on his feet, in action, being applauded by his friends and assaulted by his foes as he carried the word of reason and understanding to all who would hear and heed him. Even in death, he was teaching us—proving through his martyrdom the stupidity and futility of violence and venom—and proving, as he had always maintained, that the extremists of left and right, each busily denouncing the other, in reality fear reason and hate truth far more than they fear and hate each other.

He would remind us now that there is "a time to be born and a time to die"—but in our grief over the grotesque prematurity of his death we could not believe this was his time to die. There was so much more he wanted to do. He so dearly loved his family and his work and life itself—he had so narrowly escaped death twice before—and he had, as he said so often, quoting Robert Frost, "promises to keep and miles to go before I sleep." How, then, could it be that he should be taken from us when he stood on the very threshold of the promised land to which he had led us?

Kennedy was young, some may say—did he not die too young and too soon to be a major figure in history? The answer is all about us. We have not forgotten Byron, Keats or Shelley. We do not now regard as incomplete the music of Schumann or Schubert, the art of Van Gogh or Van Dyck. No—nor did the religion founded by Joseph Smith, or the continent explored by Henry Hudson and Meriwether Lewis, or the philosophies devised by Thoreau and Pascal and Kierkegaard, perish with their untimely deaths.

Yet still the thought remains that he had so little time. And it is true that the administration of John Fitzgerald Kennedy was not even given three years to bring the light of his love and learning to his countrymen and to the world.

The ministry and administration of John Fitzgerald Kennedy, in little more than a thousand days and a thousand nights, breathed new spirit and new quality into every aspect of American life. He wasted no time and he wasted no opportunities.

No other President in history did so much to show friend and foe alike the suicidal futility of nuclear war and the enduring possibilities of peace.

No other President in this century did so much for human rights and the recognition of human dignity.

No other President in this century achieved so much legislation for the health and the education of Americans.

No other President in peacetime history ever achieved so great and rapid an increase in our capacity to deter aggression and defend freedom.

No other President in peacetime history ever presided over so great and rapid a growth in our national income and output.

No other President in our time did so much to summon the American people to The Realities of their responsibilities.

And, finally, no other President in our time did so much to bring hope to the world—hope for a life of decency, hope for a world of peace, hope for the American destiny.

He was a man of his time—and the times demanded such a man. Without his patience and strength, the hostile missiles in Cuba might never have been withdrawn, the Test-Ban Treaty might never have been signed, the Peace Corps might never have been created, outer space might never have been peacefully explored, and all the new and compassionate programs, which are so little known but for which he worked so hard—for the mentally ill and retarded, for the unemployed and the underpaid, for the very young and the very old, for brighter cities and better farms, for more parks and playgrounds and public works—all these might never have been enacted.

All this and more John Kennedy did. Who are we, therefore, to say that his life was incomplete or his promise unfulfilled? We have reason to be proud and grateful—proud that we elected him President, grateful that we had him three years.

But pride and gratitude can only go so far—and they cannot hide our sorrow. For today the one overriding thought is still the fact that he is gone—his wit and his wisdom, his cool mind and his warm heart, his gaiety and his grace, all are gone. And we must complete the voyage he charted.

"And (so) the stately ships go on
To their haven under the hill,
But O for the touch of a vanished hand
And the sound of a voice that is still."

A Tribute
to
John F. Kennedy

Harry Golden,
The Carolina Israelite, Charlotte, N.C.,
November-December, 1963

The Irish say very seriously they are descended from Irish kings. Probably in the old days there was a king every ten miles or so, and every one gathered under each king's protection was related to him by ties of blood.

The old Irish legends tell of tall men, full of grace and dignity, brave, wise; generously giving of themselves for the good of all. These were the kings of Ireland.

They seemed only legends until we were given one of their sons for too brief a time. Now we know the legends are true. We can send down words telling of noble deeds that will become legends in their turn of a great and beloved leader, John Fitzgerald Kennedy, worthy son of kingly forebears.

Peter Lisagor,
Chicago Daily News,
November 23rd, 1963

T he enormity of the assassin's crime left hundreds of millions here and throughout the world numb with shock.

But the shock didn't hit me until later, much later.

I was one of many reporters with President Kennedy in Dallas, and only some wavering instinct kept me going through the routine of a job after we knew that some tortured mind had shot John F. Kennedy.

My first reaction was one of total disbelief, and then shame. I shared this shame with a receptionist in the clinic at the Parkland Memorial Hospital. She tried, bless her, to get a telephone call through to Chicago for me.

As she struggled with the dial, she looked up at me. Her eyes were haunted with shame. "Why Dallas?" she asked, her voice tight with tension, "Why Dallas?" And she turned her head away, sobbing.

Even now, back in the capital, where people are still staggered by the crime, it is difficult for me to adjust—and to remember. My notes are a ganglia of tangled words, heard, scrawled, repeated on a telephone, and then suddenly undecipherable. It doesn't matter. I don't need those notes. I will never need them.

I didn't come unravelled, really, until we were flying home from Dallas late Friday evening. I had agonized through an assignment to do a piece about the Johnson administration, what it might be like, what turns it might take, etc.

I finished it on a plane plunging through a night of unreality, and then it hit me. The Johnson administration? What was I doing, playing games?

Where was John F. Kennedy? What had happened to the young man with the wheat-colored hair, who had stood against long odds in 1960 and gone for broke with a flourish, who a few hours earlier had sat in an open limousine with his beautiful wife and received with broad smiles the greetings of the thousands in the streets?

John Kennedy had once said that "life is unfair." It seemed an easy abstraction then, but now . . . now, did he have some premonition that it could prove to be unfair to him too?

My mind turned back . . . to the morning and a light rain that didn't dampen the spirit of the crowd gathered in the parking lot across from the Texas Hotel in Fort Worth. The President virtually skipped out, all smiles, shook hands as usual, quipped about Mrs. Kennedy arranging herself in her hotel room.

"It takes longer," he said, "but of course she looks better than we do."

Then at a Chamber of Commerce breakfast in the hotel, Mrs. Kennedy made a belated, breathtaking appearance in a pink suit, with hat to match. The President remarked he had the "sensation" of feeling that he was accompanying Mrs. Kennedy through Texas. "Nobody wonders what Lyndon and I wear," he laughed. And the crowd laughed with him.

Not until much later did I remember that Vice President Lyndon B. Johnson paused near Hugh Sidey of *Time* magazine and me during the Fort Worth parking lot rally. I reached out and tapped him on the arm, and Hugh and I said in unison, "Hello, Mr. Vice President."

23

He looked around, spoke quickly, "Hello there," shook hands, and turned away.

"He doesn't want to talk about Texas politics," I said, but in a moment he was working the crowd with handshakes as vigorously as the President.

A few minutes later, the President was given a 10-gallon Texas hat as a gift and urged to try it on. But he always hated what the photographers call "baloney" pictures. But he did say, in what turned out to be a deeply and sadly ironic remark, "I'll put it on in the White House on Monday and if you'll come up there, you can see it then."

Within hours in the brilliant sunshine of Dallas, this vibrant young man, his mission unfulfilled, would lie mortally wounded. And Lyndon B. Johnson would be the new President, head of a Johnson administration.

I could strike a typewriter, sound coherent on a telephone, pursue an old routine with a mindless detachment. But then I knew shock, and could remember that John Kennedy liked to say that change is the law of life.

Mary McGrory,
Washington Star

Of John Fitzgerald Kennedy's funeral it can be said he would have liked it.

It had that decorum and dash that were in his special style. It was both splendid and spontaneous. It was full of children and princes, of gardeners and governors.

Everyone measured up to New Frontier standards.

A million people lined every inch of his last journey. Enough heads of state filed into St. Matthew's Cathedral to change the shape of the world.

The weather was superb, as crisp and clear as one of his own instructions.

His wife's gallantry became a legend. His two children behaved like Kennedys. His 3-year-old son saluted his coffin. His 6-year-old daughter comforted her mother. Looking up and seeing tears, she reached over and gave her mother's hand a consoling squeeze.

The procession from the White House would have delighted him. It was a marvelous eye-filling jumble of the mighty and the obscure, all walking behind his wife and his two brothers.

There was no cadence or order, but the presence of Gen. de Gaulle alone in the ragged line of march was enough to give it grandeur. He stalked splendidly up Connecticut Avenue, more or less beside Queen Frederika of Greece and King Baudouin of Belgium.

The sounds of the day were smashingly appropriate. The tolling of the bells gave way to the skirling of the Black Watch Pipers whose lament blended with the organ music inside the Cathedral.

At the graveside there was the thunder of jets overhead, a 21-gun salute, taps, and finally the strains of the Navy hymn, "Eternal Father Strong to Save."

He would have seen every politician he ever knew, two ex-Presidents, Truman and Eisenhower, and a foe or two. Gov. Wallace of Alabama had trouble finding a place to sit in the Cathedral.

His old friend, Cardinal Cushing of Boston, who married him, baptized his children and prayed over him in the icy air of his Inaugural, said a low mass. At the final prayers, after the last blessing, he suddenly added, "Dear Jack."

There was no eulogy. Instead, Bishop Philip M. Hannan mounted the pulpit and read passages from the President's speeches and evoked him so vividly that tears splashed on the red carpets and the benches of the Cathedral. Nobody cried out, nobody broke down.

And the Bishop read a passage the President had often noted in the Scriptures: "There is a time to be born and a time to die." He made no reference to the fact that no one had thought last Friday was a time for John Fitzgerald Kennedy to die—a martyr's death—in Dallas. The President himself had spent no time in trying to express the inexpressible. Excess was alien to his nature.

The funeral cortege stretched for miles. An old campaigner would have loved the crowd. Children sat on the curbstones. Old ladies wrapped their furs around them.

The site of the grave, at the top of one slope, commands all of Washington. Prince Philip used his sword as a walking stick to negotiate the incline.

His brother, Robert, his face a study in desolation, stood beside the President's widow. The children of the fabulous family were all around.

Jacqueline Kennedy received the flag from his coffin, bent over and with a torch lit a flame that is to burn forever on his grave—against the day that anyone might forget that her husband had been a President and a martyr.

It was a day of such endless fitness, with so much pathos and panoply, so much grief nobly borne that it may extinguish that unseemly hour in Dallas, where all that was alien to him—savagery, violence, irrationality—struck down the 35th President of the United States.

Joseph Alsop,
New York Herald Tribune,
November 25th, 1963

Of all the men in public life in his time, John Fitzgerald Kennedy was the most ideally formed to lead the United States of America.

Such, at any rate, is this reporter's judgment, perhaps biased, but at any rate based on long experience and close observation, and no longer possible to suspect as self-serving. To be sure, judging Kennedy was never easy, for he was no common man, to be judged by common standards.

Courage, intelligence, and practicality; a passion for excellence, and a longing to excel; above all, a deep love of this country, a burning pride in its past, and an unremitting confidence in the American future—these were the qualities which acted, so to say, as the mainsprings of Kennedy the President.

Kennedy the man, Kennedy the private face, was half the enemy and half the reinforcement of Kennedy the President. He had an enviable grace of manner and person. He enjoyed pleasure. After Theodore Roosevelt, he was the first American President to care for learning for its own sake. After Abraham Lincoln, he was the first American President with a rich vein of personal humor—which is a very different thing from the capacity to make jokes.

This strange, dry, detached, self-mocking humor no doubt aided him to assess men and events; but in his public role, it was a handicap. Certainly it was not the same sort of handicap as Lincoln's humor, which actually prevented great numbers of otherwise intelligent persons from taking Lincoln seriously.

President Kennedy's humor instead inhibited him from showing the depth of his feelings. Any public exhibition of emotion gave him gooseflesh. So foolish people said he was a cold, unfeeling man, although few men in our time have had stronger feelings about those things that mattered to him.

After his country, what mattered most to him was to live intensely, with purpose and effect. He was in some sense the ultimate personification of the observation of Justice Holmes: "Man is born to act; to act is to affirm the worth of an end; and to affirm the worth of an end is to create an ideal."

The ideal that Mr. Kennedy affirmed in action was singularly simple; for no man was ever more contemptuous of the theological complexities of ideology. (It was hard to know, indeed, whether he held a more sovereign contempt for the doctrinaire mushiness of the extreme American left or for the doctrinaire hate-preachings of the extreme American right. He was slow to anger, but these made his gorge rise.)

His ideal could be completely summed up in only a score or so of words—a nation conceived in liberty and dedicated to the proposition that all men are created equal; the proud stronghold of a new birth of freedom; and the standing promise to all men that Government of the people, by the people and for the people shall not perish from the earth. The noble, ancient phrases, the pieced-together tags from the finest of all American utterances, are as well-worn by now as antique coins, whose legend is illegible. But *He* could read the legend still. *He* still took this definition of our Nation's purpose with perfect literalness; and this was the ideal that his actions sought to affirm.

Whereas Franklin Delano Roosevelt took office when the Nation was clamoring for leadership and crying out to be shown a new course, John Fitzgerald Kennedy took office in a time of violent—yet hardly comprehensible—change.

Too many, then as now, confronted the vast revolutionary processes of our time either with fatty complacency or with shrill, embittered indignation. His task was therefore a hard task, and he was untimely cut off before his task could be half done.

Yet if we look at our country and the world in which we live —if we honestly compare the prospects now opening before us with the prospects as they seemed when Mr. Kennedy's presidency began—we can see that there has been a new birth of hope.

It is perhaps pardonable, at this moment, to be personal. Speaking for myself, I have not dared to hope as I do now since those first months of the Korean War, when such overly high hopes were born from a strong sense that America was grandly accomplishing a high, historic service. That service had its heavy price.

I still remember watching the wolfhound regiment through a long, hard fight, and how the bodies of the fallen were carried in when the fight was won, and how I suddenly could think only of Simonides' epitaph that was inscribed, for all to read, on the tomb of the dead Spartans at Thermopylae. The dead speak:

Go, stranger, and in Lacadaemon tell
That here obedient to the laws we fell.

But the President who is lost to us, like those men who were lost in Korea so many years ago, was no drilled, unthinking Spartiate. He was the worthy citizen of a Nation great and free —a Nation, as he liked to think, that is great because it is free. This was the thought that always inspired his too brief leadership of our republic.

Ferdinand E. Marcos,
President of the Senate of the Philippines,
Manila Bulletin, November 26th, 1963

Death is the greatest of tragic poets. For in a moment it captures the essence of life and distills its emotion, an achievement to which poetic language may only vainly aspire.

In a few moments of shock, on the report of his death, the whole of mankind glimpsed the life and purpose of John F. Kennedy. The hearts of men pounded in unison their cadence of sorrow; great chords of sympathy seemed to arise all over the world as from a universal cathedral.

Death, like the poet, in condensing life by that same alchemy also expands it. Kennedy's death opened a mysterious spring that flooded the world in an instant with the intimacy of his beloved presence and the sudden void on his departure. Each one of us responded as though he belonged to us, too, and his loss therefore was our own.

31

Art Buchwald,
New York Herald Tribune,
November 26th, 1963

We weep . . .

We weep for our President who died for his country.
We weep for his wife and for his children.
We weep for his mother and father and brothers and sisters.
We weep for the millions of people who are weeping for him.
We weep for Americans, that this could happen in our country.
We weep for the Europeans.
And the Africans.
And the Asians.
And people in every corner of the globe who saw in him a hope
    for the future and a chance for mankind.

We weep for our children and their children and everyone's
    children.
For he was charting their destinies as he was charting ours.

We weep for the Negro who saw in him a chance for a decent
    life.

We weep for the workingman for whom he tried to find jobs.
We weep for the artist and the writer and the poet—
For he cared about all of us.

We weep for the teachers and the pupils;
We weep for old people whom he tried to help.
We weep for the young people whom he believed in.
We weep for the soldiers and sailors and airmen whom he commanded.
We weep for their parents because he saved their children from being destroyed by war.

And while we weep, we weep for the twisted mind that committed this horrible crime;
We weep for all the tortured and warped people who could not accept the decent things he stood for.
And we weep for all the hatred and prejudice that fill the hearts of such a small segment of our society.
We weep because there is nothing else we can do.

33

Art Buchwald,
New York Herald Tribune,
November 26th, 1963

$\mathbf{A}$mong the many qualities of the late President Kennedy was his magnificent sense of humor. He had the timing and touch of a master comedian and when he was on a program with professionals he always put on a better show than they did.

John F. Kennedy had great humor about himself.

One of his famous lines was delivered at a Gridiron Dinner when he was still a Senator in 1958. He read a telegram from his father which said: "Dear Jack—Don't buy a single vote more than is necessary—I'll be damned if I'm going to pay for a land-slide."

Another famous line had to do with the criticism of his brother, Bobby Kennedy, whom he appointed Attorney General. "I was criticized about appointing my brother Attorney General—but I don't see what's wrong with giving him a little experience before he goes out to practice law."

He kidded about his religion. He said at his last Gridiron Dinner: "I asked the Chief Justice of the Supreme Court whether he thought our new educational bill was constitutional and he said, 'It's clearly constitutional—it hasn't got a prayer.'"

Mr. Kennedy was most at home joking about politics. He delighted in kidding those who opposed him.

Once in Columbus, Ohio, he received a rousing ovation at a dinner and when it finally died down he said, "There isn't a town in America where I get a bigger hand and a smaller vote than Columbus, Ohio."

During the campaign in 1960 he spoke at an Al Smith dinner given by Cardinal Spellman. In his opening remarks he said, "Cardinal Spellman is the only man so widely respected in American politics that he could bring together amicably, at the

same banquet table, for the first time in this campaign, two political leaders who are increasingly apprehensive about the November election, who have long eyed each other suspiciously, and who have disagreed so strongly, both publicly and privately —Vice President Nixon and Governor Rockefeller."

At a fund-raising luncheon: "I could say I'm deeply touched, but not as deeply touched as you have been coming to this luncheon."

When ex-President Truman suggested the Republicans could go to hell and Vice President Nixon objected to the profanity, Mr. Kennedy said he sent Mr. Truman a wire. "Dear Mr. President, I have noted with interest your suggestion as to where those who vote for my opponent should go. While I understand and sympathize with your deep motivation, I think it is important that our side try to refrain from raising the religious issue."

President Kennedy was hard put to restrain his humor at his press conferences.

A White House aid told us before every press conference the President made up outrageous answers to some of the questions.

Once the President said, "It's very dangerous to have these ideas in the back of my head."

At every press conference he managed to call on one or two women reporters to relieve the tension. Once when he addressed the first meeting of the President's Commission on the Status of Women he said, "We have established this commission for two reasons. One is for my own self-protection. Every two or three weeks May Craig asks me what I'm doing for women."

One of the late President's lines, which today has lost all its humor, was, "It has recently been suggested that whether I serve one or two terms in the Presidency, I will find myself at the end of that period at what might be called an awkward age —too old to begin a new career, and too young to write my memoirs."

Bill Baggs,
The Miami News,
November 23rd, 1963

The face was so young as it thrust across America and searched for the favor of the voters . . . and the voters, barely enough of them, a critic might add, smiled or nodded at the face . . . and he was elected the President of the United States of America, and that was in 1960.

Not long ago, when a visitor looked across the desk at the President, the face seemed to have grown old. It was not so much the new wrinkles. And maybe it was not age at all. Perhaps a philosopher, studying the mood of the face, might say that John Fitzgerald Kennedy had learned a great sorrow, which was that the soaring optimism of bold young men cannot quickly batter down the ramparts of bold prejudices within the country or suspicions among nations.

You guess, or you believe, there is wisdom in such sorrow.

Go back to a day almost three years ago when the face was young and untroubled. Maybe naive. But resolute. A friend sat at the luncheon table in Palm Beach and asked Joseph P. Kennedy why his son . . . wealthy and esteemed and free of great burdens, really . . . would wish to take on the presidency.

The father replied that he had wondered the same thing, and he said his son had told him that great challenges come along in a generation and someone in the ranks of the generation must take on these challenges. Joe Kennedy said his son had explained to him he thought he knew the challenges of our time and was willing "to accept the challenge" for his generation.

The times on this old green planet had served up to the new President two crises.

One was about civil rights. The Negroes of America had been promised emancipation almost a century before, and they were not yet free. The other crisis had to do with The Bomb.

As the new President put it, it was the obligation of his generation to "get the genie back into the bottle."

Mr. Kennedy got intimate with these two crises. Not since Abraham Lincoln has a president enlisted all his authority to open the doors for the Negroes of the land, and this was tough work, which disturbed many Americans, and just as tough, though a bit more remote from Americans, was the work to brush aside the hard suspicions abroad by arranging a treaty to stop the poisoning of the earth by ending the tests of nuclear weapons.

These are the two issues, or crises, which touch the heads of all our children, and perhaps J.F.K. wore sorrow on his young face because he knew these two great troubles had really not been solved . . . but only a beginning had been scratched out to solve them.

Yet it is the beginning on this agonizing trouble at home and on the hope to thwart nuclear war which are the credentials our young President carried with him into history yesterday.

For those who live on, Mr. Kennedy has left an obligation to finish what he began. The sorrow which had grown into the face of our young President, the wise sorrow it seemed, insists that Americans try.

Raymond Aron,
Le Figaro, Paris,
November 23rd, 1963

I always found him straightforward, unpretentious, intelligent. He listened with an extreme eagerness, he caught your point even before you had finished expressing it. He leapt at ideas. For this professional politician, according to the accepted expression, had a passion for understanding which was no less than his passion for acting. Of each of his visitors he asked suggestions with real modesty, convinced as he was that one man must decide but only after having listened to the others. He wanted to be one of the statesmen whose names are recorded in history because they accomplished a task, because they guided a nation beyond the movements or moods of crowds. I imagine that to the question: Which is the quality that you value most highly? He would have answered: Courage. It was not given to him to reach the end of his ambitions and to achieve his vocation fully. But the first Roman Catholic President of the United States, and one of the youngest, will leave a memory which will not be unworthy of the grandeur which he dreamed of attaining.

Excerpt from letter
from Mrs. William I. Elliott, Yokohama, Japan,
sent to Mrs. Helene Nelson,
Chicago, Illinois

Immediately when there came the news of Mr. Kennedy's death, there was a silencing of life here and then a siege of grief as I have never seen before and never thought possible in Japan. No one told the Japanese to be shocked: they just cried with pain and anger and sorrow, as if the human psyche had been slammed in a car door, and maimed. Some thought of phoning us to express their grief; some did phone; some wrote letters; some merely bowed on the streets or on the trains (such as the conductor); some approached but didn't speak; one man cried in my arms; some observed silence in our presence; some flew flags, Japanese and/or American, at half-mast. Interestingly, of the roughly a dozen Americans I've talked to since the death, all of them admitted that they cried and that all of their friends cried too. I would find it difficult to grasp how it would be possible not to cry.

"That Was The Week That Was,"
British Broadcasting Corporation,
November 23rd, 1963

The reason why the shock was so great, why when one heard the news last night one felt suddenly so empty, was because it was the most unexpected piece of news one could possibly imagine, it was the least likely thing to happen in the whole world. If anyone else had died, Sir Winston Churchill, De Gaulle, Khrushchev, it would have been something that somehow we could have understood and even perhaps accepted, but that Kennedy should go, well, we didn't believe in assassination any more, not in the civilized world anyway.

When Kennedy was elected three years ago, it was as if we'd all been given some gigantic, miraculous present. Suddenly, over there in Washington was this amazing man who seemed so utterly right for the job in every way that we took him completely for granted. Whenever we thought about the world, we had that warm image at the back of our minds of a man who would keep everything on the rails. Now suddenly that present has been taken away from us when we thought we had still five more years before we need start worrying again.

When the news came through shortly before eight o'clock last Friday night, more than a thousand people all over London caught buses or tube trains, took taxis, drove or walked to the American Embassy in Grosvenor Square. They had to do something. In Berlin, Mayor Willy Brandt asked people to put lighted candles in their darkened windows. Within minutes they were flickering all over the city. In Moscow at five past eight the radio broke into its programs to announce the news. It was followed by solemn organ music. In London viewers reacted with equal hostility to being treated to a half hour of comedy or being deprived of twenty minutes of soap opera.

42

"I Still Can't Believe It"

© 1963 HERBLOCK
THE WASHINGTON POST

When Kennedy was picked to be Democratic candidate in 1960, Norman Mailer wrote a piece about him in *Esquire* called "Superman Comes to the Supermarket." At that time, of course, the general opinion was that Kennedy was too perfect, too good to be true, a PRO's ideal American. He had all the film star image, a beautiful wife, great speeches with easy quotations from Burton and Shakespeare, and the ice cold efficiency, respect for the facts, but there was the homely-all-American humanity of the man who, when he went out on family boating picnics and his wife went down into the boat eating the *pâté de foie gras,* was sitting quite happy in the bow knocking back the peanut butter sandwiches.

But once Kennedy was in office the dream came true. Behind the rocking chair and the cultural evenings at the White House and Caroline's pony and the parties in Bobby's swimming pool, behind the trappings of the image was the first western politician to make politics a respectable profession for thirty years, to make it once again the highest of the professions and not just a fabric of fraud and sham. When most statesmen die they have to be explained away with words like "integrity" and "cunning" and "courage," but Kennedy did not need such apologies for he was simply and superlatively a man of his age, who understood his age; who put all his own energy and the best brains of his country into solving its problems and who ended up in more cases than not by doing the right thing at the right time because he had gone about it in the right way.

Herb Caen,
San Francisco Chronicle,
November 25th, 1963

It is less than 72 hours since the shots rang out in Dallas, yet it seems a lifetime—a lifetime of weeping skies, wet eyes and streets, and emotions that couldn't always be kept in check. Americans are not, by nature, an emotional people; the San Franciscan prides himself on an unflagging gaiety. And yet, over the endless weekend, San Francisco looked like a city that was only slowly emerging from a terrible bombardment. Downtown, on what would normally have been a bustling Saturday, the people walked slowly, as in shock, their faces pale and drawn, their mood as somber as the dark clothes they wore under the gray skies.

I remember a famous picture, early in World War II, of a Frenchman crying uncontrollably on the Champs Elysées as the Germans marched into Paris; some people found the photo painfully moving, others criticized him for not keeping a stiff upper lip in the face of the Hun. A grown man doesn't cry in public: It is part of the American lexicon.

But we are affected variously by various tragedies, and there were grown men crying in San Francisco—the stinging tears of sorrow and frustration. It was already the day after, but it took

45

only a quick reminder to bring the grief back to the surface.

A man walked past the blacked-out corner window of the City of Paris, with its small white card of tribute, and tears rolled down his cheeks. At Sixth and Mission, an old woman in black passed a late newspaper headline, and suddenly sobbed. At the opera house Saturday night, Sir Malcolm Sargent and the Royal Philharmonic of London opened the concert with "The Star-Spangled Banner," and the sense of loss was felt again; all over the house, tears glistened afresh.

The longest weekend, that was to have been the big game weekend, and never have perspectives been so suddenly shattered, never have day-to-day values come in for such an excruciating reappraisal. The few people in the downtown bars sat hunched over their drinks, staring down or straight ahead. For once, in the Nation that loves humor, there was none. All at once, a city had stopped smiling.

Gray skies, and the constant gray and black of the TV screen. For the first time, in these unprecedented hours, there was total television. You were irresistibly drawn to the tiny screen, as though you expected a miracle. But there were no miracles, only the minor miracle of three networks striving valiantly, and with commendable dignity, to transmit hour after hour of unfolding tragedy, symbolized by a flag on a coffin. You were immersed in a fantasy world of honor guards standing at attention in the rain, of endless streams of black limousines, of faces that suddenly became part of your life, and to whose familiar voice and manner you clung, as though seeking reassurance. . . .

For some of us, who spend too much time at our jobs and our pleasures, and too little exploring the manifestations of greatness, the weekend provided an awakening. As always, it came too late. For those of us who seldom have the opportunity to watch TV, John F. Kennedy became more alive in death than he had been in life. For hour after hour, through the marvel of electronics, we saw the President as though for the first time. His life, compressed onto the small screen, passed before our eyes, and we marveled at his spirit, his warmth, his humor, his brilliance. He seemed vibrantly alive, and his words had a life they never seemed to possess before. We drew strength from him, and, in a way difficult to define, hope. But the lump in the throat refused to be downed.

As you watched the fine young man, the utter senselessness of the tragedy that had snuffed out his life gnawed at you. There was not even a mad nobility in the act, no glimmer of even an insane purpose. This had not been a madman in the mold of John Wilkes Booth, leaping onto the stage of a theater, crying "Sic semper tyrannis!" This was not the inevitable gloomy grandeur from which Greek tragedy is forged, nor the uncontrollable furies of Shakespeare. This had been a warped young man—"a loner," they called him—who kept saying he didn't do it. In the confusion of his own life, he symbolized nothing. Or perhaps he symbolized nothing but confusion, and that itself is a symbol of the times.

And so today, a Nation already in shock goes into official mourning, and Arlington prepares to receive another fallen soldier. He died without knowing how much he was loved—or by how many.

John Masefield,
poet laureate
of England

All generous hearts lament the leader killed,
The young chief with the smile, the radiant face,
The winning way that turned a wondrous race
Into sublimer pathways, leading on.

Grant to us Life that though the man be gone
The promise of his spirit be fulfilled.

William Attwood,
Look,
December 31st, 1963

I never knew Jack Kennedy very well. I was not what they called a New Frontier insider or even an old friend. Over the past four years, I don't think I talked with him more than twenty times. So do not read on if you are expecting one of those intimate portraits.

I knew him as a boss—and he was a darn good one. You knew where he stood and what he wanted. You could always get to him when you had to, and when you did, you knew that he was interested in what you were doing and in what you had to say. I've just been looking at a note he sent me a few weeks before he was killed. He simply wanted to let me know he'd read an article I'd done for *Look*, and had liked it. And at the end he wrote, "Many thanks."

Many thanks. Well, I think perhaps it's my turn now to thank Jack Kennedy. Not for any personal favors—I don't mean that. He did make me ambassador to Guinea, and I spent a couple of hard and satisfying years there, but I'm not thanking him for that. What I'm grateful for is something not as tangible: It's for having made me and my generation—some of us, anyway—feel alive, exhilarated and prouder to be Americans than we've ever been before.

This is no small thing. It takes a lot to give you this kind of feeling when you're past forty and have, as they say, been around.

The funny thing is that Jack Kennedy seldom acted as if he were trying to inspire or stir up the people who worked for him. Maybe that's why he succeeded. Maybe we reacted to him and to his style of doing things because he was always cool, always restrained, always himself, and never, in the slang of our generation, corny.

I remember flying into El Paso on his plane during the 1960 campaign. It was night and we were late, and a crowd of 7,000 people had been waiting at the airport for hours. They wanted to yell and cheer, and they wanted him to wave his arms and smile and say something about the Texas sky and stars. But he just strode out of the plane and jabbed his forefinger at them and talked about getting America moving again. And then he turned and climbed into a car and drove away.

A few days later, when I saw him on the plane, I told him the crowd had felt let down and suggested that the next time he should at least wave his arms the way other politicians did and give people a chance to get the cheers out of their throats. Kennedy shook his head and borrowed my notebook and pencil (he was saving his voice for the day's speeches) and wrote, "I always swore one thing I'd never do is—" And he drew a picture of a man with his arms in the air.

Jack Kennedy could never pretend to be somebody he wasn't. He couldn't even put on funny hats or Indian feathers like other candidates. He had his own personal, downbeat style, and all who met him got used to it, and the country got used to it, too.

It was a style that had class—in the very best sense of that word. In Boston, where he started the long political journey that ended in Dallas, they loved him for it. Outside an Irish tavern on East Broadway in Boston, after President Kennedy died, a court clerk named Patrick Hines was trying to talk away his tears:

"Oh, I remember when he used to come marching down this street in a parade, and boy, he had that walk, and no hat, and 'My name is Jack Kennedy, I'm a candidate for Congress,' and girls used to flock around him—young, young, personality second to none—God, we'll miss him!"

Outside of Boston, I don't suppose many Americans had yet learned to love him the way they loved FDR or Ike (I'm sure he was embarrassed by the affection of those who did)—but even his political opponents liked and respected him, and that's what he really wanted.

Jack Kennedy was cool, but not cold. He sought the Presidency, he used to say, "because I want to get things done," and he was anything but cool and detached about these things, these measures that he believed would make America stronger and the world safer. . . .

He was tough, too, and God knows we needed a tough President as we entered the sixties. I first glimpsed his toughness a few weeks before he was nominated. We were having dinner in Washington. I had been doing some work for Adlai Stevenson, and Kennedy wanted to know why Stevenson was holding back, instead of supporting him for the nomination. I told him that some of Stevenson's friends thought the convention might deadlock, and they wanted him to be available, just in case. Also, people were talking about a Stevenson-and-Kennedy ticket.

Kennedy dismissed this possibility: He had the first-ballot votes all but sewed up, and if by some chance he couldn't make it, he would never settle for anything else. He was running for the Presidency, period.

I started to say something about how some people thought he wouldn't refuse the second spot if it came to that, but he cut me off in mid-sentence. His eyes were cold and his voice—as flat as a slap—ended the conversation: "Yes, well, you can tell them they're wrong."

I have a feeling that the Soviet Ambassador saw that look and heard that voice during the Cuban crisis last year, just before the Russian ships turned around in mid-Atlantic. . . .

He was respected around the world because he was trusted—

and because of him, those of us privileged to represent our country in the world were trusted too. It was a wonderful time to be an American abroad. How often I can remember being able to say, with pride, in Africa, "I know this is what President Kennedy believes—this is what we Americans stand for." I remember the foreign minister who told me: "Let me know what we can do to help your President. We need him as much as you." And I remember, at the United Nations in New York, the day he died, all the African hands gripping mine, the eyes full of tears.

He talked the language of the young leaders of this turbulent new world because, in his mid-forties, he was one of them. I saw some of these leaders at the White House and talked to them later. They thought of him as a friend. He knew their problems and made them understand ours. It was because of President Kennedy, because they had talked to him and knew what he was trying to do, that the leaders of Black Africa have been so understanding of the torment and the violence of our own struggle for freedom and equality here at home.

Out in the world, Jack Kennedy's memory will also live on, for years to come, wherever the Peace Corps is, for that was his idea and, I suspect, one of the most enduring legacies of his Administration. For the Peace Corps volunteers, I'm sure, as for most of us who were serving overseas when he was President, it was good to know he was back there in the White House, cheering us on, in his own way, by making the decisions and fighting for the legislation that would help us in our work.

Like Harry Truman, he could make up his mind, and he didn't pass the buck. He made you want to try harder because you knew he was trying all the time. Those of us who worked for him usually felt we were hitting on all cylinders, and glad to be. He often spoke of the ancient Greeks' definition of happiness—"the exercise of vital powers along lines of excellence in a life affording them scope"—and some of us were able, under his leadership, to appreciate that definition for the first time. And I'm grateful for that. . . .

And now, with Christmas almost upon us, I find myself

thinking of last Christmas and the present I brought back to my 11-year-old daughter from the White House. It was a note from the President in answer to a letter she had written him. She had it framed, and it has been on her bedside table ever since. The note is signed, "Your friend, John F. Kennedy."

She never met the President, but she always thought of him as her friend, and she was crying that terrible weekend because her friend was dead.

This Christmas, I think a lot of Americans, like my daughter, feel they have lost a friend. They have.

Monsignor Francis Quinn,
The Monitor,
November 29th, 1963

Last Monday, young John, you saluted your father on the way to his burial.

It was your third birthday and you could not understand. But you did well to salute him. And someday you will understand why.

Someday you will understand that God gave to your father all the qualities that other men admire.

Your father had exceptional intelligence. We marveled at his grasp of facts and his clarity of expression.

He seemed to have a natural compassion for all people. It just wasn't in him to be small in dealing with others. He was the kind of man who would have had compassion even for his assassin.

Though he was rich he was one of us.

Though he had every reason to, he never took himself too seriously.

He was young, and our civilization puts great store on youth.

God had given him handsome features and an attractive personality.

He was a man of straightforward religious faith. He attended

55

Mass as easily and unaffectedly as he did everything.

He was apparently the kind of father all fathers want to be—loving you and your sister and loved by you.

More than anyone else in our memory your father seemed to have all the qualities we expect in a hero.

And with it all he had a humility which enhanced everything else.

To all appearances God had been unbelievably generous to your father. But to whom much is given, much is asked.

A man like this doesn't just happen. He is forged out of suffering and sacrifice.

God had asked him to carry many crosses. He had suffered the loss of a brother and a sister in the prime of life. He had seen another sister burdened with a serious affliction. He had been called to endure heroic hardship in a World War. In illness he had come so close to death he was anointed. As a father he had suffered the loss of your brother Patrick.

In his chosen profession he had assumed a job at a time in history when the burdens were enough to break the back of any man.

Though he served in an arena where deeds are sometimes sordid and principles ignored, this was a man demanded by his times.

Like you will be in a few years, young John, the world today is awkward. It is an adolescent asked to grow up faster than it can. It needed a leader with intelligence far above the average; it needed a youth to keep up with the jet-speed times; and most of all it needed someone with stability to temper the wild currents that are sweeping across the world and the passions inflaming the hearts of men.

He helped us in bewildering times.

You do not understand any of this now. But may you salute your father all through your life. May you do more than that.

Please, God, may you resemble him.

Norman Cousins,
Saturday Review,
December 7th, 1963

An American President is something special in the world precisely because American history has been something special. A nation founded on a decent respect for the opinions of mankind is bound to attract reciprocal sentiments. And when an American President gives life to the central purpose built into the design of that nation, the purpose being to advance the human cause on earth, it is natural that profound feelings of human oneness should be released. No matter that the purpose may have been dented or even battered through crisis or contention. Enough of it is left to produce a response, especially at a time of national tragedy.

The Japanese farmer and his family who walked eighteen miles through the night in order to stand silently in front of the American Embassy in Tokyo; the Warsaw bus driver who, upon being informed by a boarding passenger of the terrible news, halted his vehicle and wept openly; the elderly woman in Dublin who cried because her own body could not have intercepted the bullet; the students who carried memorial torches in Berlin; the long lines of grieving people who gathered outside official American stations or residences in London, Paris, Rome, Berlin, Moscow, Mexico City, Toronto, Athens, Istanbul, Beirut, Tel Aviv, Cairo, Teheran, New Delhi, Madras, Karachi, Leopoldville, Conakry, Tananarive, Hiroshima, and a hundred other cities; and the people everywhere who could only sit quietly with their sorrow— all this is more than a world expression of sympathy. It is a reminder of what this country is all about. It makes real the connections, seen and unseen, between the United States and the human community—connections that were basic in the thinking of the men who fashioned this nation.

John Fitzgerald Kennedy had immersed himself in history long before he made it. He had studied the American experience and written about it. When he moved to the White House he didn't superimpose himself upon American history; he fitted into it just as it fitted into him. He didn't have to wander through government archives looking for records of ideas and acts that had gone into the making of the American purpose. This knowledge was part of him and he put it to work. . . .

At his command was immediate obliterative power, more power by far than had ever been collected in one place at one time. In the American arsenal were thousands of explosives, some of which contained more force than all the bombs and shells in all the previous wars in history put together. In toto, this destructive force represented the equivalent of 30,000 pounds of TNT for every human being on earth.

He regarded this power not as a source of true security, for, as he said, a nation's security could shrink even as its atomic might would expand. The power—not in our hands alone but in the hands of other nations—had to be brought under world control. It could not be unilaterally discarded—this would not create safety or sanity; it would have to be eliminated as part of a genuine world security system under law.

In this sense, John F. Kennedy as President was confronted with issues involving human destiny. Woodrow Wilson used to say that his constituents included the next generation. The question before John Kennedy was whether there would be a next generation at all—here or elsewhere. This for him was not a melodramatic fact; he was not the melodramatic type. But it was a fact nevertheless and it never left him. He knew that his job was connected to the whole of the human future. No greater burden had to be sustained by any man in the history of the race. . . .

John Kennedy came into office at a time when most of the world's peoples were shopping for a revolution. He knew he had to identify the United States with the desire for freedom of a billion people; he had to make this identification convincing to those who were then or had been under the domination or control of the nations with whom the United States had been closely linked for almost two centuries. He did everything he could to accelerate the historical process of national freedom. But he knew, too, that the issues went beyond independent statehood; it had to do with a conception of man himself. Did man own himself? Was government instituted to protect and cherish the concept of individual sovereignty, which is to say, a free man? Or was man a unit in a vast organism to which he was subordinate and secondary? In either case, man had to be fed, housed, educated, developed. These needs were insistent. Which ideology had most to say to him? . . .

Wisdom begins with the ability to make valid distinctions. John Kennedy made distinctions not just between one part of an ideological camp and another but within each camp itself. He knew that the Soviet Union was in a process of profound historic transition. He made distinctions between its dominant character and thrust under Josef Stalin and its dominant character and thrust under Nikita Khrushchev. The combination of the total irrationality and total power possessed by Stalin permitted no sensible dialogue under which reasonable and workable limits might be set to the struggle between the Soviet Union and the United States. Nikita Khrushchev was hard but at least he was rational. He could be expected to take advantage of every opening in order to advance his national interest but he was not deranged. He had no eagerness to see the Soviet Union incinerated in a nuclear war.

John Kennedy's policy, therefore, was to close off every possible opening through which the Soviet Union might advance its national or ideological interests to the detriment of other nations, and to keep open every channel through which sensible arrangements by the two countries might be made in their joint interest and in the human interest. One example of this policy was Cuba. Another was the nuclear test ban. Both seemed to point in starkly opposing directions, yet both were part of the same basic purpose; that is, a determination to resist encroachments and a determination to explore every opportunity to build a durable peace.

This policy was never better articulated by the President than in his June 10, 1963, American University commencement talk. With the possible exception of his September 20, 1961, talk before the General Assembly, the American University address was the most historic and important human document of his three years in office. The June 10 speech was an attempt to face new realities. It tried to cut through the insanity of mounting nuclear stockpiles and mounting antagonisms. It tried to apply a human perspective to grave international problems. It tried to speak directly to the Russian people, not lecturing or scolding but giving full weight to their ordeals and difficulties and recognizing that common hopes can dissolve even the oldest enmities. The full text of this talk was published in the Soviet press.

The June 10 talk led in a straight line to what was perhaps the President's greatest triumph in the foreign policy area. This was the successful fight, in his words, to get the nuclear genie back into the bottle. He had to obtain Soviet adherence to a nuclear test-ban treaty and then he had to obtain Senate ratification, and he did both. He regarded this treaty not just as an end in itself but as a possible wedge into far more difficult and consequential problems between the two countries.

Questions of human destiny, world political upheaval, and ideological struggle were not the only burdens carried by the young President. Inside the United States, another historic process was approaching its culmination. The American Negro was emancipated from slavery but not from humiliation. He received his liberation but not his rights. He was not so much freed as cast adrift. He was accorded no place of essential opportunity or dignity. And the same groundswell that a hundred years earlier had culminated in what another martyred President had called a fiery ordeal was beginning to make its tremors felt.

People today forget that Lincoln was condemned by many of his contemporaries because he didn't move faster, because he seemed to temporize, because he spent so much energy on persuasion. But Lincoln knew his main job was to hold the country together, appealing to reasoning people on both sides and trying to effect a profound transition without insanity or national tragedy. . . .

The same men who have no hesitation today in acclaiming Lincoln for his leadership on the issue of human rights have no difficulty in denouncing John Kennedy for acting as Lincoln acted. John Kennedy tried to find an answer, not to force a solution. His job, no less than Lincoln's, was to keep even the bitter and basic issues from producing a national convulsion. He knew that fundamental questions of human rights could not and should not be deferred any longer. And he accepted the need to find every opening, develop every resource, command every initiative in that direction. But always in front of him, to paraphrase Madison, were the purifying but enfeebling limitations to the Presidential office in bringing about fundamental change. . . . The original design for the Presidency had called for a proper number of checkpoints on the executive power, but it never anticipated that ultimately the checks and pressures would multiply to the point where the President would spend most of his life running a gauntlet.

"The laws," wrote De Tocqueville, "allow a President to be strong but circumstances keep him weak." Confronted with these circumstances, some Presidents sought to delegate authority to the greatest possible extent. John Kennedy had some buffers, to be sure, but he knew that he had to carry the main burden himself for putting through his program. . . .

The key to John Kennedy was that he was in the American rationalist tradition. Not every problem had an answer but every problem had its origins and component parts, each of which called for weighing and grading, and all of which were related to one another in a way that increased the probability of a workable answer. Even when he felt justified in making a summary judgment, he would feel more comfortable if someone he trusted went over the ground again.

John Kennedy would have no trouble in qualifying for inclusion in the kind of company Carl Becker wrote about some years ago in a striking book called *The Heavenly City of the Eighteenth Century Philosophers*. The men who founded the United States are among the principal characters in the book. They were men of reason and believed in the uses of history. What were some of the articles of their faith? A good government was distinguished from bad to the extent that it can develop a memory and put it to work. Tyranny and injustice were likely to recur if the conditions that favored tyranny and injustice recurred. Good men might retard or even combat the effects of the tyranny, but it was much more rational to avoid the cause. Even good men had a tendency to go bad under certain circumstances. Therefore, do everything possible to alter the negative circumstances and create the propitious ones.

The "heavenly city" of the American founding fathers was a condition of enlightenment in which human intelligence and rational thought could be addressed to the perfectibility of man and human society in general. This environment, like man himself, was highly delicate and had to be carefully nurtured. The result was an ingenious system under which the individual had greater protection against excesses or encroachments by officialdom than existed almost anywhere else on the face of the earth.

But the design was not without its inevitable flaws. The rationalist founding fathers did everything they could to protect the individual against government, but they had no way of protecting government against the irrational individual. One man with a gun could create chaos, could shatter the brain of the man whose decisions were critical to the life of that community, and could lay a burden of grief on the hearts of millions.

Confronted with this fact, some people now wonder whether the rational design ought not somehow be changed. Some may even say that the design is no longer workable. John Kennedy would be the first to remind them that not even the most totalitarian society can protect itself altogether against a man with a gun. Indeed, with his sense of history, he would be certain to point out that totalitarianism almost automatically fosters such violence, for that is often the only way to change it.

Is there then nothing we can do to halt and expunge the obscene and spreading violence? Is there no way to keep the face of the nation from being pock-marked and blistered by men putting their tempers to triggers? Is the shape of America to be determined by a barroom brawl?

There is something we can do.

We can re-examine the indifference to violence in everyday life. We can ask ourselves why we tolerate and encourage the glorification of violence in the things that amuse us and entertain us. We can ponder our fascination with brutality as exhibited hour after hour on television or on the covers of a thousand books and magazines. We can ask why our favorite gifts to children are toy murder weapons.

We can ask whether we are creating an atmosphere congenial to the spiraling of violence until finally it reaches a point where living history is mauled and even our casualness toward it is pierced.

We can resensitize ourselves to the reality of human pain and the fragility of human life.

There is something else we can do at a time of emptiness and national deprivation.

We can be bigger than we are. We can rise above the saturating trivia, redefine our purposes, and bring to bear on problems that combination of reason, sensitivity, and vision that gives a civilization its forward movement. Our ideals are all right, W. Macneil Dixon once said, but they are unreal until they become articulate.

We can give not just added protection but added dignity to public office and reduce the sense of loneliness of public servants who are regarded as easy game for the predatory attacks of extremists.

The best defense against spiraling madness is to carry on, to strengthen the belief in a rational society and in the natural sanity and goodness of man, to take all reasonable precautions but not to allow the precautions to distort or disfigure our lives. "The fact that reason too often fails," Alfred North Whitehead said, "does not give fair ground for the hysterical conclusion that it never works."

The sense of tragedy over the assassination of the President will not soon be dispelled, but in due time we may find warrant for some consolation in the fact of orderly succession, a miracle in itself, built into the structure of government. Even more basic is the fact that there is nothing to stop the American people from giving life to the ideas and purposes of the man whose memory they now cherish. The loss of John Kennedy becomes a total one only if our understanding of what he tried to do is emptied from our minds.

One of the unique characteristics of a free society is that it can assign immortality to a concept, an ideal, a set of working principles. If the impact of John Kennedy is confined to the circumstances of his death, then the tragedy is indeed a total one. But if there is accord with his purposes, then this may be a solvent for our grief. This, then, is the time for brave and reasonable men to come out of hiding. And this is the time to put ideals to work.

John Kennedy believed in peace. He believed in freedom. He saw no conflict between the two. He believed in the creative potential of the individual man. He believed in the reality of hope. He relished laughter and the vigorous life of the mind. He loved life, and by life he did not mean segregated life; he meant all life. He believed in thought. He believed in reasonable exchange. He recognized obligations to people not yet born —to help provide them with a good earth and a decent world.

The ultimate tragedy of a man is represented not by death

but by the things he tried to bring to life that are buried with him. The legacy of John Kennedy can be a large one—if that is the way the American people wish it to be.

Miraflores,
November 26, 1963.

D̲ear Caroline and John-John:

I am very sad with the death of your father. He was a great man and a friend of mine whom I much liked and esteemed. He worried a lot for the poor people not only of the United States but of Latin America; that they could go to school, live in decent houses and have health centers to cure their illnesses. That is why among the two hundred millions of men and women that make up the population of Latin America there were many people who loved and esteemed him. His death has been much lamented and millions of beings have wept for him.

As you may remember, my little Caroline, your father took you by the hand to the door of the White House so that you and I could meet. It was a demonstration of friendship that your father gave me and which I shall always remember.

I kiss you both, and may God bless you.

(signed) Rómulo Betancourt

To
Caroline and John-John Kennedy
Washington, D.C.

pete, El Tiempo, Bogotá, November 27th, 1963

DOS HUERFANOS — Por Chapete

Letter from
Doctor Albert Schweitzer
to Mrs. Joseph P. Kennedy,
December 19th, 1963

Mrs. Joseph P. Kennedy
200 Park Avenue
Suite 3021
New York, N.Y., U.S.A.

Dear Mrs. Kennedy:

It touched me deeply that you want for members of your family, books autographed by me. I received the books today and send them back to you on this same day.

I want to tell you about the role which your son, President Kennedy, played in my life. Einstein, the great scientist and I were great friends since we were young. When the atomic bombs commenced operating, we at once pronounced ourselves against it.

Einstein died, desperate because he protested against these horrible weapons without any success. I went on fighting. I waited year after year, if not a great political personality would sincerely occupy himself with this terrible danger for mankind.

In course of time, I became conscious that it was President Kennedy. This was a great consolation to me.

When the Moscow Treaty was published, I saw a ray of light

again in the darkness. I felt prompted to congratulate your son and my congratulations touched him. I was sure that the two big powers could cooperate for freedom.

And now it happened that your son, who could have been the saviour of the world, fell a prey to a fanatic. I do not know who could have his clear-sightedness, his tenacity and his authority in order to continue his great political and humanitarian work.

At present, we walk in the darkness again. Where are we going? Your son was one of the great personalities of history in the world. Millions of us mourn with you.

Yours deeply devoted,
/s/ Albert Schweitzer

Docteur Albert Schweitzer
Lambarene, Gabon,
West Equatorial Africa
19.12.1963

Theodore H. White,
Life
Memorial Edition

She remembers how hot the sun was in Dallas, and the crowds—greater and wilder than the crowds in Mexico or in Vienna. The sun was blinding, streaming down; yet she could not put on sunglasses for she had to wave to the crowd.

And up ahead she remembers seeing a tunnel around a turn and thinking that there would be a moment of coolness under the tunnel. There was the sound of the motorcycles, as always in a parade, and the occasional backfire of a motorcycle. The sound of the shot came, at that moment, like the sound of a backfire and she remembers Connally saying, "No, no, no, no, no. . . . "

She remembers the roses. Three times that day in Texas they had been greeted with the bouquets of yellow roses of Texas. Only, in Dallas they had given her red roses. She remembers thinking, how funny—red roses for me; and then the car was full of blood and red roses.

Much later, accompanying the body from the Dallas hospital to the airport; she was alone with Clint Hill—the first Secret Service man to come to their rescue—and with Dr. Burkley, the White House physician. Burkley gave her two roses that had slipped under the President's shirt when he fell, his head in her lap.

All through the night they tried to separate him from her, to sedate her, and take care of her—and she would not let them. She wanted to be with him. She remembered that Jack had said of his father, when his father suffered the stroke, that he could not live like that. Don't let that happen to me, he had said, when I have to go.

Now, in her hand she was holding a gold St. Christopher's medal.

She had given him a St. Christopher's medal when they were married; but when Patrick died this summer, they had wanted to put something in the coffin with Patrick that was from them both; and so he had put in the St. Christopher's medal.

Then he had asked her to give him a new one to mark their 10th wedding anniversary, a month after Patrick's death.

He was carrying it when he died and she had found it. But it belonged to him—so she could not put that in the coffin with him. She wanted to give him something that was hers, something that she loved. So she had slipped off her wedding ring and put it on his finger. When she came out of the room in the hospital in Dallas, she asked: "Do you think it was right? Now I have nothing left." And Kenny O'Donnell said, "You leave it where it is."

That was at 1:30 p.m. in Texas.

But then, at Bethesda Hospital in Maryland, at 3 a.m. the next morning, Kenny slipped into the chamber where the body lay and brought her back the ring, which, as she talked now, she twisted.

On her little finger was the other ring: a slim, gold circlet with green emerald chips—the one he had given her in memory of Patrick. There was a thought, too, that was always with her. "When Jack quoted something, it was usually classical," she said, "but I'm so ashamed of myself—all I keep thinking of is this line from a musical comedy.

"At night, before we'd go to sleep, Jack liked to play some records; and the song he loved most came at the very end of this record. The lines he loved to hear were: *Don't let it be forgot, that once there was a spot, for one brief shining moment that was known as Camelot."*

She wanted to make sure that the point came clear and went on: "There'll be great Presidents again—and the Johnsons are wonderful, they've been wonderful to me—but there'll never be another Camelot again.

"Once, the more I read of history the more bitter I got. For a while I thought history was something that bitter old men wrote. But then I realized history made Jack what he was. You must think of him as this little boy, sick so much of the time, reading in bed, reading history, reading the Knights of the Round Table, reading Marlborough. For Jack, history was full of heroes. And if it made him this way—if it made him see the heroes—maybe other little boys will see. Men are such a combination of good and bad. Jack had this hero idea of history, the idealistic view."

But she came back to the idea that transfixed her: *"Don't let it be forgot, that once there was a spot, for one brief shining moment that was known as Camelot*—and it will never be that way again."

As for herself? She was horrified by the stories that she might live abroad. "I'm *never* going to live in Europe. I'm not going to 'travel extensively abroad.' That's a desecration. I'm going to live in the places I lived with Jack. In Georgetown, and with the Kennedys at the Cape. They're my family. I'm going to bring up my children. I want John to grow up to be a good boy."

As for the President's memorial, at first she remembered that, in every speech in their last days in Texas, he had spoken of how in December this nation would loft the largest rocket booster yet into the sky, making us first in space. So she had wanted something of his there when it went up—perhaps only his initials painted on a tiny corner of the great Saturn, where no one need ever notice it. But now Americans will seek the moon from Cape Kennedy. The new name, born of her frail hope, came as a surprise.

The only thing she knew she must have for him was the eternal flame over his grave at Arlington.

Watercolor by Mrs. Kennedy
Hammersmith Farm, October, 1961.
From the President's Office

"Whenever you drive across the bridge from Washington into Virginia," she said, "you see the Lee Mansion on the side of the hill in the distance. When Caroline was very little, the mansion was one of the first things she learned to recognize. Now, at night you can see his flame beneath the mansion for miles away."

She said it is time people paid attention to the new President and the new First Lady. But she does not want them to forget John F. Kennedy or read of him only in dusty or bitter histories:

For one brief shining moment there was Camelot.

Benjamin Bradlee,
Newsweek, December 2nd, 1963

Histroy will best judge John F. Kennedy in calmer days when time has made the tragic and the grotesque at least bearable. And surely history will judge him well—for his wisdom and his compassion and his grace.

John Kennedy was a wonderfully funny man, always gay and cheerful, never mean—but historians are prone to stifle laughter in formality. You could see a laugh coming in his eyes before you could hear it from his lips. His humor was often most appealing when he directed it against himself. One summer night in a Georgetown garden, candidate Kennedy was preparing for the first of many critically important appearances on "Meet the Press."

"You be Kennedy and I'll be Spivak," he suggested to his guest with relish, and the first question was already spilling forth: "All right, Horatio Alger, just what makes you think you ought to be President?"

Only days ago, his thoughts turned to the farewell party for a White House aide who had been memorialized in print as "coruscatingly" brilliant. "Those guys should never forget," he said with a smile, "50,000 votes the other way and we'd all be coruscatingly stupid."

John Kennedy was a forgiving man, far more forgiving than his friends. He forgave many the excesses of their ignorance—many men who hold high positions today because of this forgiving. He forgave quickly and for good, and soon found new quality in the forgiven.

John Kennedy was a hungry man, ravenous sometimes for the nourishment he found in the life he led and the people he loved. This was both literally and figuratively true. He could eat ten bowls of specially prepared fish chowder without succumbing either to indigestion or embarrassment, and though he smoked only rarely, he could chain-smoke three cigars when the spirit moved him. His ability to devour the written word was legendary, and he could unwrap presents faster than a 5-year-old.

John Kennedy was a graceful man, physically graceful in his movements—walking, swimming, or swinging a golf club—and had that special grace of the intellect that is taste. He never told a dirty joke. He could not bring himself to be "corny" at a time when "corniness" is a hallmark of American politics. On his next to last trip, to the American wilderness, this compleat and urbane man was uncomfortable in the clothes of a conservationist; and he laughed loudest of all at the "Paul Bunyan" or "Johnny Appleseed" nicknames he quickly collected. During the 1960 campaign he used the phrase "Jackie and I" only once, and that was enough to embarrass him. He was a student of graceful expression, and had been since he started collecting rhetoric in a small, black leather book before the war.

John Kennedy had a Walter Mitty streak in him, as wide as his smile. On the golf course, when he was winning, he reminded himself most of Arnold Palmer in raw power, or Julius Boros in finesse. When he was losing, he was "the old warrior" at the end of a brilliant career, asking only that his faithful caddy point him in the right direction, and let instinct take over.

John Kennedy was a restless, exuberant man, always looking forward to the next challenge. For a year now, it had been "Wait till '64" more and more often. And for a long time he had wondered—at first in fun but increasingly in seriousness—what he would do after his second term. He wondered if he might become the editor of a newspaper. He had no real doubt that he would be re-elected—hopefully with the mandate that he missed so much after the 1960 election, the kind of mandate that would let him do what he thought the country needed done.

He wanted to run against Goldwater (though he liked Goldwater personally more than he liked Rockefeller), and settle forever the dangers he saw in standing still. John Kennedy was a blunt man, sometimes profane, when it came to assessing rivals. But in his judgment, no man was all bad who had run for political office, and by the same token, every man would be better if he ran for political office. He bore no man lasting grudge or envy, and his readiness to love was instinctive.

For John Kennedy was a loving man, lately come to lasting love. And historians are too far removed from love.

John Kennedy reveled in love for the Irish patrimony that he had left so far behind. He laughed with love at the roguery of his grandfather, Honey Fitz, and his trip to Ireland was a pilgrimage to that love.

He loved his brothers and sisters with a tribal love. All Kennedys were born gregarious, but under siege it could be the Kennedys against the world.

John Kennedy loved his children with a light that lit up his world. He discovered his daughter when election brought them finally under the same roof, and he delighted in her pride and in her performance. His heart leapt up when he saw his son, careening through life as if there were no tomorrow, and he lit up the hearts of all who saw them enjoy each other.

And John Kennedy loved his wife, who served him so well. Their life together began as it ended—in a hospital—and through sickness and loneliness there grew the special love that lights up the soul of the lover and the loved alike.

John Kennedy is dead, and for that we are lesser people in a lesser land.

Saint-John Perse,
Le Monde, Paris

No myth of history, he. Among us, without mask, he was a man simple, close and warm, prompt to meet the action of each day, carrying his live ammunition to every challenge in the community.

An athlete, he ran races to encounters with destiny. He was a fighter, who battled in the open field and he went to his death barefaced. He marked everything with a rhythm of his own and we are left trailing his traces.

Servant of a great people, in love with liberty, holding high up the legacy of its great elders, he was also mankind's soldier, defender of all rights, of all freedoms.

No one was a greater enemy of abstraction, nor more given, by instinct, to go right to the heart of the matter: shrewd and firm in his judgment, his realism as a statesman was tempered, in his actions, by his humane sense as much as by his sense of the possible. He had the clear and straight gaze of young leaders molded out of friendship for humanity.

At a time when a great and free democracy had been, before him, threatened, for a time, by an easy paternalism, he knew how to give the alert, and rekindle, indeed bring forth a new national sense of citizenship to a point of full integration, and to militantly awaken around him a sense of moral responsibilities, individual or collective. This he did without concern for comforts in the exercise of government.

Carrying farther this spiritual solidarity, he knew how, from the heart of other people, to summon their own genius and their deep calling. Ever respectful and fervent toward France, he was awaiting with confidence, an answer worthy of his questioning.

May the light disperse the shadow before us! And may the road of history be the greater for the men honored with stelae. Lincoln upon whom Walt Whitman wept awakens in our hearts, even now, the very long span of the martyr.

When destiny carries to such a height the lightning of its thunder the drama becomes universal and the sorrow of a people becomes the sorrow of all. . . . This is a French standard I have hoisted at half the height of the mast, in mourning.

Jean-Jacques Servan-Schreiber,
L'Express, Paris,
November 28th, 1963

Kennedy, the first political leader of our age, is gone now.

He bequeaths us the example of his flashing sallies and the heritage of his failures. He leaves us on the frontier.

After all, it is natural that he was laid low by violence. He raised too many new problems, setting loose the interests attached to them and the passions which they involve.

But those who killed him will have no respite. The assassination of a pioneer gives fierce determination to the others. Money cannot buy enough killers: a crime like this will mobilize a generation.

André Fontaine,
Le Monde, Paris,
December 7th, 1963

Italy at last has a government; Turkey no longer has one. Venezuela has a new president. Once more people have begun to talk about elections in Britain: political life is progressively regaining its place. And yet, fifteen days after the assassination of John Kennedy, the stupor which seized America and the world has not worn off. Three shots have for a length of time frozen history. In the first place, they have destroyed a symbol: that of the triumph of youth. From Peking to Washington, the earth was governed by old men upon whom years had heaped wounds and disappointments which withered their hearts. And then, a man happened to enter the White House who had dash and confidence in a society which he invited, as the pioneers of yore, to expand its frontiers. The manner in which the Old World reacted to the Dallas tragedy demonstrated that this appeal was heard far beyond the United States. Beyond the natural emotion of people whom the cinema has accustomed to the intimacy of star performers, there was among millions of young and not so young men the feeling of a personal blow, of an injustice of destiny, of a revenge of blind fate.

The mourning was not only that of the Western world. For the first time since the war, the sorrow of Americans was shared by Russians. Thanks to television, the latter followed the news, minute by minute, as they had never been allowed to do in the course of their history. To date, this is the most convincing recorded indication of the progressive reduction of the mental gap separating East and West. Even the Chinese, in spite of the fact that they live in a psychological prison, seem to have understood the indecency of their reaction.

America herself felt the ordeals as a bludgeon stroke, so deeply that no one tried to exploit it on a political level. Yet God knows that the agitated past of Lee Oswald had enough to inspire fishing in troubled waters.

She has lost more than a President: a family which had given to the Republic the monarchical style indispensable to the formation of affectionate ties between a nation and its leader. Whereas she gives moral lessons to others easily, she was ashamed, profoundly ashamed, in the face of this double crime which flouts her good conscience and her faith—admirable in many respects—in her institutions. Finally, she rediscovered, in the midst of her intellectual, physical and moral comfort, the presence of death, this familiar companion of Old Europe but which people on the other side of the Atlantic had believed they could almost conjure away in the softened light and sweet music of funeral parlours. The murder of a Catholic President, the wish of his widow, bracing herself in unusual mourning crape, to give him a hero's funeral in the European manner, her will of showing herself in the first place worthy of him, were undoubtedly needed to make the nation discover that man never was so weak as at the time of his apparent almightiness. Leaders or led, the citizens of the United States dream of mathematical certainties, of all-risk insurance. The crime has shown them in a flashing second the futility of such a hope. Like human beings, societies mature. Such blows help them to do so.

Mayor Willy Brandt
of West Berlin,
November 22nd, 1963

Not only has a light gone out; no, a flame has been extinguished, extinguished for all human beings hoping for a just peace and a better life in this world. On this Friday night, the world has become much poorer. The horrible news about the death of President John F. Kennedy fills us Berliners and all honest Germans in both parts of our divided country with deep, deep mourning.

A few months ago, President Kennedy honored us in the German capital with the simple word that he was a Berliner. Berlin has lost its best friend and the first citizen of the free world. Germany will not forget John F. Kennedy.

James Reston,
New York Times,
November 23rd, 1963

America wept tonight, not alone for its dead young President, but for itself. The grief was general, for somehow the worst in the nation had prevailed over the best. The indictment extended beyond the assassin, for something in the nation itself, some strain of madness and violence, had destroyed the highest symbol of law and order.

Speaker John McCormack, now 71 and, by the peculiarities of our politics, next in line of succession after the Vice President, expressed this sense of national dismay and self-criticism: "My God! My God! What are we coming to?"

The irony of the President's death is that his short Administration was devoted almost entirely to various attempts to curb this very streak of violence in the American character.

When the historians get around to assessing his three years in office, it is very likely that they will be impressed with just this: his efforts to restrain those who wanted to be more violent in the cold war overseas and those who wanted to be more violent in the racial war at home.

He was in Texas today trying to pacify the violent politics of that state. He was in Florida last week trying to pacify the businessmen and appealing to them to believe that he was not "anti-business." And from the beginning to the end of his Administration, he was trying to damp down the violence of the extremists on the Right.

It was his fate, however, to reach the White House in a period of violent change, when all nations and institutions found themselves uprooted from the past. His central theme was the necessity of adjusting to change and this brought him into conflict with those who opposed change.

Thus, while his personal instinct was to avoid violent conflict, to compromise and mediate and pacify, his programs for taxation, for racial equality, for medical care, for Cuba, all raised sharp divisions with the country. And even where his policies of adjustment had their greatest success—in relations with the Soviet Union—he was bitterly condemned.

The President somehow always seemed to be suspended between two worlds—between his ideal conception of what a President should be, what the office called for, and a kind of despairing realization of the practical limits upon his power.

He came into office convinced of the truth of Theodore Roosevelt's view of the President's duties—"the President is bound to be as big a man as he can."

And his inaugural—"now the trumpet summons us again"—stirred an echo of Wilson in 1913 when the latter said: "We have made up our minds to square every process of our national life with the standards we so proudly set up at the beginning and have always carried at our hearts."

This is what the President set out to do. And from his reading, from his intellectual approach to the office, it seemed, if not easy, at least possible.

But the young man who came into office with an assurance vicariously imparted from reading Richard Neustadt's *Presidential Power* soon discovered the two truths which all dwellers on that lonely eminence have quickly learned.

The first was that the powers of the President are not only limited but hard to bring to bear. The second was that the decisions—as he himself so often said—"are not easy."

85

Since he was never one to hide his feelings, he often betrayed the mood brought on by contemplating the magnitude of the job and its disappointments. He grew fond of quoting Lord Morley's dictum—"Politics is one long second-best, where the choice often lies between two blunders."

Did he have a premonition of tragedy—that he who had set out to temper the contrary violences of our national life would be their victim?

Last June, when the civil rights riots were at their height and passions were flaring, he spoke to a group of representatives of national organizations. He tolled off the problems that beset him on every side and then, to the astonishment of everyone there, suddenly concluded his talk by pulling from his pocket a scrap of paper and reading the famous speech of Blanche of Spain in Shakespeare's *King John:*

The sun's o'ercast with blood. Fair day, adieu!
Which is the side that I must go withal?
I am with both; each army hath a hand,
And in their rage, I having hold of both,
They whirl asunder and dismember me.

There is, however, consolation in the fact that while he was not given time to finish anything or even to realize his own potentialities, he has not left the nation in a state of crisis or danger, either in its domestic or foreign affairs.

A reasonable balance of power has been established on all continents. The state of truce in Korea, the Taiwan Strait, Vietnam and Berlin is, if anything, more tolerable than when he came to office.

Europe and Latin America were increasingly dubious of his leadership at the end, but their capacity to indulge in independent courses of action outside the alliance was largely due to the fact that he had managed to reach a somewhat better adjustment of relations with the Soviet Union. . . .

He was, even to his political enemies, a wonderfully attractive human being, and it is significant that, unlike many Presidents in the past, the people who liked and respected him best, were those who knew him the best.

He was a rationalist and an intellectual, who proved in the 1960 campaign and in last year's crisis over Cuba that he was at his best when the going was tough. No doubt he would have been re-elected, as most one-term Presidents are, and the subtle dualism of his character would have had a longer chance to realize his dream.

But he is gone now at 46, younger than when most Presidents have started on the great adventure. In his book, *Profiles in Courage*, all his heroes faced the hard choice either of giving in to public opinion or of defying it and becoming martyrs.

He had hoped to avoid this bitter dilemma, but he ended as a martyr anyway, and the nation is sad tonight, both about him and about itself.

Gene Graham,
The Nashville Tennessean,
November 24th, 1963

What does one write whose stock in trade is political humor when the nation's President lies dead in the White House, victim of an assassin's bullet? Nothing is funny.

And yet John Kennedy, rest his soul, possessed perhaps the best developed sense of humor that ever resided at 1600 Pennsylvania Avenue. He could laugh. More, he could laugh at himself.

It was never a crude guffaw, true, simply a white flash that worked overtime splitting his square-jawed tan. The smile frequently followed one of his own quips. He was full of them.

In the most desperate times, he could call up the safety-valve mechanism of wholesome humor. He could laugh at Vaughn Meader mocking Jack Kennedy, and then outdo Meader at his own mocking trade.

In 1960, I followed Jack Kennedy across the nation, chuckling at every stop. He had the remarkable ability to project at once the image of a deeply serious young man, anxiously concerned with his country's welfare, in a terrible hurry to rescue it—and all the while with a laugh on his lips.

His wit was urbane. It lurked a hair-scratch beneath the surface and popped above at the tiniest provocation. And yet he never attracted the sort of criticism leveled at Adlai Stevenson, and even Abe Lincoln, for the same offense.

Perhaps this was because Abe didn't have TV and Adlai did. But Jack was perfect for the so-called "electronic media."

He could never hide his humor. You always knew when he was about to pull a funny. He struggled for a dead pan but couldn't hold it; the devilish twinkle of his eye and the quirk of a mouth tempted to grin betrayed his forthcoming quips.

I shall never forget one instance in Sioux City, Iowa, for it first introduced me to this Irishman's humor. He was an hour or so late, as usual, for an appointment at the municipal auditorium. The place was packed and stomping, every seat taken, when he mounted the rostrum.

This was farm country and Jack's farm record was not, in the Midwest view, the best. He had voted with Benson more than once. But bravely, if out of his bailiwick, Jack struck out on a farm message. He was touching their pocketbooks. Quiet prevailed.

"And so I awsk," Jack awsked the farmers in his best Harvardese, "what's wrong with the American farmer (fahmah, he pronounced it) today?"

He paused for the proper effect and a pin's drop hush awaited his answer. But the answer never came.

From high in the rafters another quipster stole Jack's highpoint hush and squawled in a pitiful tone.

"He's sta-a-a-arving!"

For the briefest instant the future President was frozen there, his right hand aloft in that familiar wood-chopping oratorical style. Then his hand came down and he bent in the middle.

Jack Kennedy was fractured in laughter. The audience roared with him.

The chopping motion, the devilish eye, the betraying quirk of the mouth are gone. And nothing is funny about their departure.

But there was much to laugh about in his life, which was the greater for that fact. God keep you, Jack, and your smiling Irish eyes.

Seàn Quinlan,
America, December 14th, 1963

They told us when we were boys how Cuchulain died: "And he went to a pillar-stone which is in the plain, and he put his breast-girdle round it that he might not die seated nor lying down, but that he might die standing up." Remembering now-ancestral precedents, I know that in my people instinctive prompting will ask America to grant us the right to number John Fitzgerald Kennedy among the heroes of our race.

I think of the hearts he warmed in my Irish homeland those few months ago. For heart spoke to heart when he came to us to end the great hunger and to redeem us not a little from our brooding on the past. We believe that we gave him something, too, some richer awareness that he shared with his Jacqueline, who summoned the jackets green across the "bowl of bitter tears" from the plains by the Liffey to a shield's length of earth at Arlington.

We remember the litany of the names of battles as he uncovered the flag of the Irish Brigade in the Irish Parliament.

We remember, distressed for our brother, that stripling's dash in Dublin back from the helicopter to kiss gently the gracious Sinéad De Valera. That was on the lawn of what was the Vice-Regal Lodge in the days when a Kennedy sailed downstream from New Ross, going West "to find the sun-tree growing."

We remember the ancient manuscript we gave him with its memories of Dalcassian land. One day may his son, grown strong and handsome, hear the love song from another Irish manuscript of the 8th century:

> He is a heart,
> An acorn from the oakwood.
> He is young,
> A kiss for him.

We remember the old priest watching television in the cancer hospital in Dublin and saying: "It's the people. They have taken him to their heart for pride. *Securus judicat orbis terrarum.*"

And when his daughter blossoms, her days of playing with a Connemara pony in the sunlit fields of Virginia over, may she, remembering "O'Donnell Abú" at her father's funeral, see one day the tomb of Nuala O'Donnell, last of Gaelic princesses, at Louvain.

We remember, too, how he and Jacqueline brought a glow like Canaletto's London to Washington. There was a poet at the Inauguration and there was a breath of festival, a pause for beauty, poetry and song at the White House.

He told us that there are no permanent enemies. Who knows what impulses went through his death to the great Council which is renewing the gospel in Rome. Who knows how many hearts were purified of hate as they saw new Arimatheans, Negro and white, bear his casket to its shield's length of earth. A great death quickens all life.

Someone has quoted Camus. That is well. When history places an immortal comma to one of its mysterious phrases, all literature and every archetype echo. His exemplary death adds new dimension to the foundations of love, and so he lays his head toward the yet unborn imagination of poets, and folklore is relighted. There is blood again in the diastole of myth and symbol.

All things ancestral were perfectly fulfilled—the death of the Abel who had inherited the blessing of his Founding Fathers; the riderless horse beneath his spirit; the little son saluting in grave mimesis all human descent; women with a cross; his death in Christ. John Fitzgerald Kennedy has become the seed that must flower in reconciliation. America now looks inward on unfolding light.

Gerry Murphy,
from the Irish Press

Sad indeed we were when that too soon Shannon leave-taking had to be taken. There was a void, a feeling of loss but yet there was running strongly too the conviction that this was not the last time we would welcome John Kennedy to Ireland.

As events have had it I was among the last who saw a deeply moved and lonely President wave just once again. We did not hear those last words lost in the jet engine's roar. But we did not have to; we knew just what his thoughts were as he turned a reluctant back on the country to which he longed to return.

John Kennedy pledged himself to return in the springtime on that June Saturday. When he told us all "I am going to come back" we all felt he really wanted to. And this was what impressed itself most on me; his sincerity.

Here was no thread-bare formula of words but a man speaking from his heart. When he said farewell at Shannon he told us that Bean de Valera the night before had recited to him a Gerald Griffin poem which he thought so beautiful that he wrote down the words.

And there was a great hush as President Kennedy paused for a moment. Then, with great feeling, he recited

'Tis, it is the Shannon's stream, brightly glancing, brightly glancing!
See, oh see the ruddy beam upon its waters dancing!
Thus returned from travel vain, years of exile, years of pain,

To see old Shannon's face again,
Oh, the bliss entrancing.

Mr. Kennedy paused again and added with determination: "I am going to come back to see old Shannon's face again." And how we all hoped that he would.

Here again I could not mistake the softness and nostalgia of his words when he recalled the lines of "Come Back to Erin" and told the crowd gathered to take their last farewell: "This is not the land of my birth; but it is the land for which I have the greatest affection, and I certainly hope to be back in the spring-time."

Desmond Mullan,
from the Irish Press

That fresh, warm day of June 27 when the President drove through the narrow winding tree shaded boreen from New Ross to Dunganstown was possibly the most remarkable day in his Irish tour and one which he obviously enjoyed immensely.

In the first seconds of his descent from the Presidential car President Kennedy dispelled the tension and strain and, even before greeting Mrs. Ryan with a warm hug and kiss, showed us how much he really thought of his homeland and its people.

His face was boyishly creased in that infectious smile, and as the evening wore on and he joined the feast in the centre of the yard we could see the President was truly at home. That peaceful rural scene is one that will live forever in the memories of the people of that green land.

The jokes about the "poached" salmon, the invitation to all and sundry to have a cup of tea, the good natured banter with newsmen and cameramen, the delighted appreciation of the women of Dunganstown when he spoke well of their cooking were all part of that homely scene. The President among his own and that quiet land of green fields and shady trees, under silver clouds over Dunganstown was far removed from the troubled world he left behind him.

For my own part I thought that it was a long, long cry from the Ryan home where he sat and drank strong tea, to the loneliness of the White House and worries of the world.

Frank O'Connor,
Sunday Independent, Dublin,
November 24th, 1963

John Fitzgerald Kennedy was a miracle. In three different ways he broke through age-old American prejudices against Catholics, against Irishmen and against intellectuals, and you have to have lived in America to realize how strong these prejudices are. Eleven years ago, in the bar of an exclusive Boston club, an old Bostonian said to me: "Do you know, you're the first educated Irishman I've ever met?" At that time, the American universities themselves were being crippled by the McCarthy inquisition.

Kennedy was the fine flower of that great university system. The American university took the Irish literary revival and put it fair and square on every arts course, and when we mock at young Americans who come here to study Yeats and Joyce, we are mocking at the very thing that straightened the backs of men like Kennedy, so that they no longer had to go around pretending they had a great-grandmother from Antrim and were really "Scotch-Irish."

Kennedy treated the Scotch-Irish with the same good-natured contempt with which he treated the native Irish who were afraid of James Joyce's name, and he boldly spoke of Joyce in the Dail, where previously Joyce's name had never been heard except on some debate on evil literature.

In his last speech in Texas he quoted brilliantly from a book of mine. He was not the man to be afraid of quoting some Irish writer, whom most of his audience had never heard of. He was leading the Irish in America out of a ghetto of humiliation and pretence and telling them that they were a people with a history and literature as good as the best. He was also leading educated Americans back into the field of Government from which they had been expelled by the distrust of intellectuals.

97

On Thursday night I was called to the telephone to hear: "President Kennedy is quoting from some book of yours in San Antonio, Texas"; on Friday night I was called to the telephone to hear: "President Kennedy is dead."

I wept, partly for ourselves, who have lost a man that represented not only his own country but ours; partly for America, whose black fate struck it again.

Melvin J. Lasky,
Forum Service, December 7th, 1963

W hat world leader in our time was so essentially in tune with the infinite problems that beset mankind? Not Roosevelt or Churchill or De Gaulle, not Gandhi or Nehru, certainly not Eisenhower or Adenauer or Mao Tsetung. Somehow he had come to understand not only the national necessities of his own country—to move forward on a broad liberalizing democratizing front—but also the far-away imperatives of different and distant peoples: their hopes for independence, for freedom, for equality, development and dignity. Above all, he understood the world's longing for peace: he, the most powerful single man in the world, with absurd weapons of annihilation at his push-button command. Let us beware of creating a pretty legend. Still, in his youthful authority, in his idealism and energy and luck, John Kennedy had given reality to the vague phrase about "American leadership in the world."

The proof was in the world-wide outbreak of emotion after November 22. Here was a new phenomenon, something beyond all national frontiers. In all of Europe, and also in the Afro-Asian world, there was a break-through to a feeling that here, in some sense, was their *own* President, that a leader of their own had been foully murdered. There are some, I know, who see in this only the new mechanical influence of publicity, of newspaper photography and television camera-work. I doubt whether the techniques of mass media alone could create such depth of feeling. Precisely because we live in such an increasingly mechanized society there is this deep private need in all of us to feel an authentic public emotion of love, admiration, fraternity.

Beyond the sorrow, there remains the continuity of historic forces. The wills have been read, and the executors have taken over. A new American President has assumed the political leadership of half the nations. How much will actually change in the hard practice of policy? One man had called out, "Let us begin . . . ," and another echoed, "Let us continue. . . ." If one looks at U.S. history from 1937 onwards, beginning with Franklin Roosevelt's famous "Quarantine the Aggressor" phrase, through Truman, Eisenhower, and Kennedy, one cannot but be struck by the remarkable continuity of foreign policy. When one stops to think of the economic (and moral) commitment to international aid—from F.D.R.'s Lend-Lease, Truman's Point Four, the Marshall Plan, to the Alliance for Progress—one sees that there are overmastering impulses at work here, which no one man's death can stem.

And even in the loss of death, there can be gain. Could it be that on the deeper emotional levels some kind of new universalism is emerging? Is it only of fleeting momentary significance that we can now praise famous men—and mourn for them—with no regard for national flags, passports, and anthems? I prefer to see a larger world-unifying meaning in this moment of anguish. "For a tear," said the poet Blake, "is an intellectual thing. . . ."

Robert Shaw
at Severance Hall, Cleveland, Ohio,
November 23rd, 1963

Certainly in the blackness which engulfs us all, each man is his own small island of grief—inaccessible and mute. One would not invade this privacy. But no public gathering during these hours takes place but in the light of that darkness.

Days ahead will be full of political appraisal and eulogy—but among those of us engaged in the pursuit of the creative, performing or liberal arts a special acknowledgement is in order.

We are accustomed to think of him in terms of abounding physical vitality and humor: a laughing father treading water while a five-year-old Caroline bomb-dives from the deck of a launch into the Atlantic Ocean, a driving young executive pacing the world's most critical office—clutched at the knee by a three-year-old John-John—or substitute-at-large for a game of touch football with the junior senator and the attorney general.

This is entirely fitting—but how terribly unfunny a word like "vigah" can become in a few hours.

And it is more pertinent to this place and this moment that we remember a president of the United States who felt it natural to honor poets, painters, architects, scholars and musicians

101

at his inauguration. . .

Under whose auspices Shakespeare and opera were presented to the president's cabinet in the president's home. . .

At whose invitation Pablo Casals performed Bach solo suites in the White House.

Let us remember the president who accorded new dignity and responsibility to the scholars and artists of his country. . .

For whom the life and creative produce of the mind and the spirit were unrivalled natural resources. . .

Who held scholarship and the arts as the ultimate focus of man's good-will and indispensable allies of freedom, peace and social justice.

There is not one of us who finds his employment or delight in gatherings such as these who was not enlarged by his living and diminished by his dying.

Richard H. Rovere,
The New York Review of Books,
December 26th, 1963

Iwas not one of the Washington journalists who knew him well and saw him often. Before his nomination, I knew him scarcely at all. The first time I sat down alone with him was only a few days before his election. He had had a wild day campaigning in and around Philadelphia. He had shaken so many hands that his own right one looked like raw beef. One woman, running alongside his car, had held on to his thumb to avoid losing her balance and perhaps being run over. There was a chance that it was broken. It hurt badly. Around midnight, I joined him at supper in his cabin on the *Caroline*. After getting me settled, he said, "What do you know about Taper?" I couldn't imagine what he meant. I had to ask him. "Taper," he said, "you know, the one who writes that column in the *Spectator*." I was at the time a correspondent for the London *Spectator*, and Taper was a pseudonym used by Bernard Levin, a political writer for that magazine, who has since become theater critic for the London *Daily Mail*. I told him what I knew, which wasn't very much; Kennedy said he admired Levin and would enjoy meeting him.

I had three talks with him in the White House. There were several more "Taper" incidents. "I ran into Kahn the other day," he said once. I wracked my brain. Kahn? Khan? Khanh? Herman Kahn, the thermonuclear-war man? Aly Kahn? Could it be a friend of mine, another Herman Kahn, an historian in the National Archives? Mohammed Khan of Pakistan? Who on earth was Kahn? And how, for God's sake, does the President of the United States "run into" anyone? He could see me struggling. "Jack Kahn, you must know him, on *The New Yorker*? He was in here doing a Talk of the Town story. He was talking to my secretary about my going to theaters in New York. I've been

103

wondering about the piece. Do you know when it's going to come out?" I knew nothing about it.

Another time, he seemed mildly and inexplicably upset about a *New Yorker* piece that *had* appeared—a profile of Pablo Casals by a man whose name actually was Taper, Bernard Taper. "It was interesting," he said, "but I figured it must have been written a long time ago. It wasn't up to date." Thinking fast, I assumed he meant that it had not said enough about the Casals concert in the White House. I asked him if that was it. "No, no," he said, and he went on to explain that in three or four places it had described arrangements in Casals' life that had changed in recent months. Something about his house, something about his dog. He seemed to feel that *The New Yorker* was somehow losing its grip if it couldn't be *au courant* in such matters. "Who is this Taper?" he said. I told him a bit, mentioning that this Taper and Pierre Salinger were friends, having worked together as reporters in San Francisco. He went on with something like, "What did you make of that last Norman Mailer piece?"

Once, when I felt that I had really taken up more than enough of his time, I tried to prepare the way for my leaving with what would have been a lame and elaborate opening. What I meant to say was something like this—that I would really worry about the country if I thought that its President was putting in a lot of time talking with someone like me about Norman Mailer, Bernard Levin *alias* Taper, Bernard Taper, and so forth. I forgot how it went, but I got out just a few words, like "Mr. President, I'm taking up too much of your time. I think that if . . ." "You think," he said, "that I wouldn't be much of a President if I spent much of my time this way."

Norman Mailer,
The New York Review of Books,
December 26th, 1963

What one has written about Kennedy was not reverent. Now, in the wake of the President's assassination, a sense of real woe intrudes itself. For it may be that John F. Kennedy's best claim to greatness was that he made an atmosphere possible in which one could be critical of him, biting, whimsical, disrespectful, imaginative, even out of line. It was the first time in America's history that one could mock the Presidency on so high a level, and we may have to live for half a century before such a witty and promising atmosphere exists again. So most of what one had to say, intended to have the life of contemporary criticism, becomes abruptly a document which speaks from the far cliff of a divide, from a time which is past, from history. What a sense of the abyss that the man is no longer with us, not there to be attacked, not there to be conversed with in the privacy of one's mind.

106

Molly Kazan

I think
  that what he gave us most was pride.
It felt good to have a President like that:
bright, brave and funny and goodlooking.

I saw him once drive down East Seventy-second Street
in an open car, in the autumn sun
(as he drove yesterday in Dallas).
His thatch of brown hair looked as though it had grown **extra**
  thick
the way our wood animals in Connecticut
grow extra fur for winter.
And he looked as though it was fun to be alive,
to be a politician,
to be President,
to be a Kennedy,
to be a man.

He revived our pride.
It felt good to have a President
who read his mail,
who read the papers,
who read books and played touch football.
It was a pleasure and a cause for pride
to watch him take the quizzing of the press
with cameras grinding—
take it in his stride,
with zest.
He'd parry, thrust, answer or duck,
and fire a verbal shot on target,
hitting with the same answer, the segregationists in a Louisiana

107

hamlet and a government in South East Asia.
He made you feel that he knew what was going on
in both places.
He would come out of the quiz with an "A" in Economics, Military Science, Constitutional Law, Farm Problems and the
moonshot program
and still take time to appreciate Miss May Craig.

We were privileged to see him on the worst day
(till yesterday),
the Bay of Pigs day,
and we marveled at his coolth and style
and were amazed at an air (that plainly was habitual)
of modesty
and even diffidence.
It felt good to have a President
who said, It was my fault.
And went on from there.

It felt good to have a President
who looked well in Vienna, Paris, Rome, Berlin
and at the podium of the United Nations
—and who would go to Dublin,
put a wreath where it did the most good
and leave unspoken
the satisfaction of an Irishman
en route to 10 Downing Street
as head of the U.S. government.

What was spoken
was spoken well.
What was unspoken
needed to be unspoken.
It was none of our business if his back hurt.

He revived our pride.
He gave grist to our pride.

He was respectful of intellect;
he was respectful of excellence;
he was respectful of accomplishment and skill;
he was respectful of the clear and subtle uses of our language;
he was respectful of courage.
And all these things he cultivated in himself.

He was respectful of our heritage.
He is now part of it.

He affirmed our future.
Our future is more hopeful
because of his work
but our future is not safe nor sure.
He kept telling us that.
This is a very dangerous and uncertain world.
I quote. He said that yesterday.

He respected facts.
And we must now live with the fact of his murder.

Our children cried when the news came. They phoned and we
   phoned
and we cried and we were not ashamed of crying but we were
   ashamed of what had happened.
The youngest could not remember any other President, not
   clearly.
She felt as if the world had stopped.

We said, It is a shame, a very deep shame.
But this country will go on
more proudly
and with a clearer sense of who we are
and what we have it in us to become
because we had a President like that.
He revived our pride.
We are lucky that we had him for three years.

109

Interview with Daniel P. Moynihan,
Assistant Secretary of Labor,
Television Staton WTOP,
Washington, November 24th, 1963

Y ou know the French author, Camus, where he came out at the end of his life, he said the world was absurd. A Christian shouldn't think that, but the utter sense-lessness, the meaninglessness . . . We all of us know down here that politics is a tough game. And I don't think there's any point in being Irish if you don't know that the world is going to break your heart eventually. I guess we thought that we had a little more time. So did he.

This nation will never be the same after he has been President. We are a bigger, a stronger, a better nation. I think we know more about what it is we have to be. I think we know somewhat more about how to be it. . . . For some of us you'll say it won't be the same in other ways. Mary McGrory said to me that we'll never laugh again. And I said, 'Heavens, Mary. We'll laugh again. It's just that we'll never be young again.'

John Cogley,
The Commonweal,
January 10th, 1964

T here are, first and foremost, the sheer facts of his life. He was the quintessential modern man, a product of the twentieth century, gifted with a good mind, a graduate of the most respected schools, a sophisticate, and a universally admired statesman. He had a horror of the pietistic and avoided moralism as if it were poison. (The only "un-American" traits in his character.) Yet, his Catholicity was as much a part of him as his modernity. He wore both of them as unselfconsciously and elegantly as he wore his London clothes. John F. Kennedy was a living refutation of the argument of those who used to hold that Catholicism was an anachronism in the modern age. He did not claim to be a saint, nor was he ever mistaken for one, but he was a man of faith and of steady, unspectacular loyalty to his Church. Finally, he died an authentic hero in the minds of millions of young Americans. That will go a long way toward shaping the image of Catholicism in the years ahead.

Secondly, whatever theoretical issues remain to be solved, President Kennedy showed by his career that American Catholicism as a matter of fact has long since come to terms with religious pluralism. Not even his bitterest critics ever accused him of personal prejudice, and the only serious criticism of his handling of religious issues during his years in the White House came from fellow Catholics. Certainly now the symbolic exclusion of Catholics from the highest office in the land has come to an end. Nor, after John F. Kennedy, can one imagine the nation embroiled in the kind of controversy that swirled around his candidacy only four years ago.

Finally—and this is a more controvertible personal view of mine—President Kennedy more than any other leader rescued the day-by-day politics that makes democracy possible from the disdain in which it had been held in America. Only a few years ago, there was a disturbing poll taken which showed that a very high percentage of Americans regarded politics as a dirty business unfit for their children. I doubt that a similar finding would be turned up today. For Kennedy took public pride and satisfaction in his vocation, and he did not identify his calling merely with the proposal of noble goals but also with the hard work and earthy craft necessary to turn those goals into reality. This latter meant compromise, frustration, wheels and deals, and above all the responsible use of power. And the President employed all these means shamelessly and candidly. Frequently in doing so he brought down upon his head the charge of being cynical, timid, power-hungry and shallow. Ideologues on both left and right found him anathema. Purists and utopians, who forever confuse rhetoric with leadership and propositions with proposals, frequently expressed their "disappointment" with him, though their expectations from the beginning were minimal. But lead he did, and as became clear at the time of his death, he also educated millions of people to the realities of the nuclear age.

David Gourlay,
Manchester Guardian Weekly,
December 12th, 1963

I know that the world has moved on from that tragic Dallas Friday and that all the heartfelt tributes have been paid and the memorial services held. At the same time, I still think that somehow it has not happened. I suppose by this attitude I am questioning history, for Kennedy's killing is already part of history.

For the first time in my life I think I know how the disciples must have felt when Jesus was crucified. Is the suggestion or thought blasphemous? This is not my intention. At the same time the fact remains that Kennedy's murder was a kind of modern crucifixion, short, sharp, and devastating. Its impact was universal and spoke directly to Heads of State and to ordinary folk everywhere. A particular man had been removed from our human scene at the hands of a fanatic or by the scheming of extremists who found his crusading zeal for all that was positive, hopeful, and affirmative in life hateful and dangerous.

In saying all this I am trying to relate my belief in Providence to the awful factual truth of what happens in history. I suppose this constitutes a search for a theology of history, by which I mean the full reconciliation of what happens in life with the belief in a loving God. It is never, and never has been, an easy search. The belief that "all things work together for good" in the face of earthquake, famine, private catastrophe or the kind of universal sorrow attending the death of a figure like Kennedy is never easy to hold.

Is there such a thing as a Christian view of history? Does it take all the other views seriously? How far does God protect the good and the just in this world? He did not, after all, blunt the nails at Calvary nor does He divert the flight of an assassin's bullet if it is truly aimed. All this, we say in our theological textbooks, is part of the structure and order of the universe. The natural order ensures, after all, that a ship sinks at a certain stage when it has struck an iceberg; it also ensures that reaping follows sowing, and that casting a net into a sea full of fish produces a good catch for the market.

Let us move the argument away from the mechanics of particular situations. I want to ask why it is that whenever goodness, justice, hope, and possibility are forcefully expressed in history there appears to be an almost unwritten rule in the order of things that they will be opposed, and not infrequently done to death. Is it the old cosmic battle between God and the Devil? Wasn't all that settled long ago at the Cross, once and for all?

It was—but we have to go on learning the lesson. What lesson? That the Cross, either in terms of Calvary or later versions, is never the final word on the conflict between life and death, hope and despair. Even when all that is positive, good, and strong is struck down in the ambiguities of history there springs up in the hearts of men such an awareness and certainty of what is finally right that all who have to go on living from day to day take fresh heart and courage. Are not Kennedy's aims and objects more compelling and also more universal than they ever were or could be before?

All this is not to say that we are unaware of the tragedy, the irony, or even the view that history repeats itself. But beyond all such prospects there emerges slowly and gradually, with tears and with calm certainty through the dark crying, the knowledge that all is not lost and that even death itself can become the way to greater life. This affirmation must now be committed by all men of goodwill everywhere to history, and to its ongoing paradoxes.

Walter Stewart,
Canadian Weekly, Toronto,
December 7-13th, 1963

O n a May afternoon, full of glowing sun-
shine and gracious talk, a group of dignitaries left Government
House, official residence of the Governor-General, and trooped
across the lawn to where a scrawny, 12-foot red oak tree stood
waiting to be planted. The year was 1961, the occasion the cere-
monial planting of a tree to signal the first—and, as it turned
out, only—official visit of President Kennedy to Canada. It was
not a remarkable ceremony. The president threw a few shovel-
fuls of loam before gratefully handing back the silverplated
spade; Mrs. Kennedy chatted and laughed as she waited her
turn to plant another tree nearby; Prime Minister Diefenbaker
and Governor-General Vanier smiled benignly. The leaders ex-
changed polite compliments about growing friendship between
our two nations and the group soon straggled back to Government House. Later, it turned out that President Kennedy had
wrenched his back, vulnerable from injuries received overseas
during World War II, and the newspapers were able to make a

116

few paragraphs out of it, but after that, the tree was forgotten.

But then the U.S. leader was assassinated, and his tree took on new meaning as a living symbol in Canada of a man now lost to the world. The afternoon of his murder—an afternoon of chill mist and blowing rain in Ottawa—Patty Johnston, chief gardener at Government House, went down to take another look at the Kennedy tree. It stands about two feet higher than it was when the president planted it but, behind the bronze plaque that marks it, the tree still looks rather scrawny and forlorn. Patty walked once around it and, reaching out, took one brown leaf and gave a little tug. It didn't come off; Patty grinned. All around, maples stood bare, but the Kennedy oak waved leaves that somehow became tattered brown flags protesting stubbornly against the onslaught of winter and, somehow, Patty's little pilgrimage seemed a fit way to remember President Kennedy.

Professor Charles Malik
of the American University of Beirut, Lebanon,
November 24th, 1963

In the presence of death we become serious and pensive. We cannot then depend on words and feeling and imagination. We demand to know the real meaning of existence. Our heart burns for the ultimate things.

Ordinarily we live forgetful of death, we live as though we were immortal; indeed, we are always trying to avert the very thought of death like death. And then death strikes like a thief in the night and we are suddenly brought to our senses. Blessed are those whose eyes death opens, and thrice blessed those who do not wait till then to remember that they are dying; for it makes no difference if you die in a year or six and forty or a hundred: you are dying.

John Kennedy was with us yesterday but today he is no more. He is no more so far as we who are left behind are concerned. Immortality may be proved although it is a fitter topic for faith; but while the impossibility of immortality may also be believed, it can never be demonstrated.

John Kennedy was with us yesterday, and what a presence he filled! The size of his presence is indicated by the simple fact that when it was lifted the whole world felt the loss. It is difficult to find another instance in history of a man whose death was as universally mourned, or another living man today whose absence all men are likely to feel. This measures not only the stature of the man but the stature and influence of the country that elected to place the man at its head.

Irish and Catholic by descent, Boston and Harvard to the core, Jack Kennedy, after receiving the finest education the United States can offer, first fought valiantly and was decorated in the Second World War, then served as a newspaper correspondent, then wrote books on world affairs, then represented the State of Massachusetts in the Federal Legislature, first as Congressman, then as Senator, and finally was raised three years ago to the highest office in the land. I had the honor of knowing the man, and what strikes you most in him, besides his wit and his disciplined mind, is his charming self-consciousness, his youthful bashfulness, and the evident sense that here is a man who is and who knows that he is destined for great things.

For two years and ten months Jack Kennedy was the President of the United States. His speeches are models of cadence and composition, studied by college students everywhere. He introduced style, brilliance, form, élan, into United States policy. He felt he had a special mission for the betterment of social and class conditions in the United States, and he bravely acted on this feeling. He was the champion of the small and weak, both nationally and internationally, and he wanted the United States to be the disinterested helper of the small nations towards development, stability and self-confidence. He was a firm supporter of the United Nations, and no head of state ever expressed the same emphatic faith in the world body as President Kennedy did.

But above all he was the knight of peace. He craved peace, he fought for peace, he sought peace with all his heart and mind. The latest and perhaps best expression of his basic outlook was his remarkable Commencement Address at The American University in Washington last June. He was fully conscious of the infinite responsibilities resting upon the United States as the major nuclear power of the world. Therefore, said his heart to him, let the issue of the cold war be decided, not on the battlefield, but through peaceful competition in peace: this was his most secret and his most sacred desire. He conferred with Mr. Khrushchev in Vienna; he succeeded, by resoluteness and wisdom, in averting a world disaster last year in connection with Cuba; he agreed with Mr. Khrushchev on setting up a "hot line" between Washington and Moscow; and he crowned his endeavors last summer with concluding the historic test-ban treaty. If the world breathes a little more freely today because the nightmare of nuclear war has slightly lifted, it is principally

119

thanks to the determined efforts, often in the face of the greatest of odds, of John Fitzgerald Kennedy. Had it been within the design of Divine Providence to lengthen his days we could not tell what further significant strides toward peace and concord this young giant among men might have taken.

But America is a great democracy ultimately governed, not by men, but by law. The Constitution provides for all eventualities, and the moment John Kennedy died Lyndon Johnson succeeded him as President of the United States. The people are never without a head and a President, and now President Johnson, having been the closest associate of Mr. Kennedy, and with his suavity and sense of humor, his roots in the southland and his great qualities of leadership, will doubtless follow in the footsteps of the late President in the relentless pursuit of peace, justice and freedom. Thus the business of the Republic goes on uninterrupted and secure.

Jack Kennedy loved his family, and the scenes of him playing with Caroline and Jack Junior in the White House or on its lawns will never be erased from the memory of his countrymen. He was also a man of faith, believing in God and taking part in the Sacraments. If only one had inner eyes to see he would discern a spiritual quality in everything he said and did.

Responsible public life is full of hazards. This is never more so than in this turbulent age. All serious men who embark on it know what they are in for. Not every man can stand it because not every man is willing to pay the high personal price it calls for. The safe and sheltered live a much securer life, but, pray tell me, who makes it secure for them? Certainly not they themselves, because if everybody seeks the broad and easy way, there will be nobody to set the pace, nobody to provide the pattern, nobody to lead and inspire and direct and give strength. It is the fate of the few, indeed of the exceedingly rare, to risk their lives that the many may live. The many, in their sheltered and frightened lives, do not know how much they owe the few who hazarded everything—their name, their nerves, their very necks—and who ended by paying with their lives, in order that some vision of truth and beauty and freedom and decency may touch the earth. And the utmost the many can rise to is, after the few and the rare have passed on, to raise monuments for them. Nor does this always happen.

If you think all it takes to scale the heights is ambition, then I suggest you try your hands at this game. If ambition alone sustains you, then you will begin to get cold feet from the second day. It takes much more than ambition to attain and lead and be and swim, especially in a sea full of sharks. It takes courage, and it is this more than anything else that distinguished the life of John Fitzgerald Kennedy. No wonder the title of one of his books is *Profiles in Courage*. There is no place for the timid among the great. Courage is when you doggedly rest in the truth preferring it to life itself; nay, Truth is Life, and all so-called "life" is but the veriest death apart from truth. Hence to die in the truth and for the truth is the only true way to live.

He who converses with the gods, he who listens to the deepest music of the ages, often most hidden and most concealed, he who welcomes solitude with all its terrible sufferings and temptations and finds in it sources of joy and creativity that the world can never know, he who ruthlessly decides for or against, himself being already decided for by something above himself, he whose destiny is to play with destiny under some transcendent lure, he whose vital roots penetrate to the truth itself, where he beholds things face to face, such a one, called to a task, will never shirk it because of danger or hazard or risk. And from the light that he sheds on the way, and from his blood that he may have to spill some day, issue blessings untold and the manna of heaven.

In this hour of grief and sorrow in which the whole world is in deep mourning, let us not think only of the dead and departed because he is now safely beyond the veil; for he is already among the immortals, both here and beyond, and no thought of ours can alter his place or avail him or us anything, save only to bow our heads in deep respect for the divine will.

Let us rather think of a beautiful woman in Washington of four and thirty years of age whose sorrow and grief it is the hardest thing for a human being to imagine or bear.

121

Let us think of two wonderful children, a boy and a girl, left now fatherless for the rest of their lives.

Let us think of a father, already old and tired in his body, who will now go down to the grave utterly broken and sad.

Let us think of a mother who put so much love and affection, so much care and devotion, into a son who turned out such a promise and such a fulfilment, but who is now no more.

Let us think of brothers and sisters and relatives and friends who are now scattered like sheep without a shepherd, a shepherd who was only yesterday the very apple of their eyes.

Let us think of a whole nation which only yesterday took great pride in its leader, a leader so gallant, so youthful and manly, so dedicated and resolute, but one who is no longer there to lead.

And let us think of the world, of you and me, who only yesterday could not think of the international scene without Jack Kennedy, without the man who to the best of his lights spared not his life that his fellow men might have some hope, some certainty, some assurance, that all is not dark and desperate ahead.

"As for man, his days are as grass: as a flower of the field, so he flourisheth.

"For the wind passeth over it, and it is gone; and the place thereof shall know it no more.

"But the mercy of the Lord is from everlasting to everlasting upon them that fear him, and his righteousness unto children's children;

"To such as keep his covenant, and to those that remember his commandments to do them." (Psalm 103:15-18)

One of the landmarks of the Washington area is Mount Vernon, the estate of George Washington. When you visit there they take you on a tour; they show you where Washington was born, the bed in which he died, the chair in which Martha his wife used to sit and knit; and then they take you to his tomb less than a hundred yards away. You stand before the tomb and look inside the iron door; the whole thing is absolutely simple, like everything genuinely American; there is no elaborateness whatever either about the sepulchre as a whole or about the marble coffin in which the body of the founder of the United States lies in peace. But what do you read above the coffin as an epitaph? What was it that George Washington wanted people to read when they looked at his tomb?

You read these old, familiar, simple words, full of mystery and meaning and hope, and you read nothing else:

"I am the resurrection, and the life: he that believeth in me, though he were dead, yet shall he live: and whosoever liveth and believeth in me shall never die." (John 11:25-26)

America therefore is founded on faith—faith in the Living God. There is nothing in the whole world—no evolution, no revolution, no change—that is going to alter this fact. Let us therefore humbly but confidently say with David:

"Give unto the Lord, O ye mighty, give unto the Lord glory and strength.

"Give unto the Lord the glory due unto his name; worship the Lord in the beauty of holiness.

"Sing unto the Lord, O ye saints of his, and give thanks at the remembrance of his holiness.

"For his anger endureth but a moment; in his favour is life: weeping may endure for a night, but joy cometh in the morning." (Psalm 29:1-2 and Psalm 30:4-5)

T ragedy is the difference between what is and what might have been. That is why the death of John F. Kennedy is one of the most authentically tragic events in the history of nations. Across the ages we hear many a cry of grief at the premature extinction of young and vivid talents. "The beauty of Israel lies pierced on the high places" sang King David of his young comrade Jonathan, slain on Mt. Gilboa. "For Lycidas is dead, dead ere his prime. Young Lycidas and hath not left his peer." So Milton mourned his boyhood friend. But neither the Hebrew warrior nor Milton's friend was cut off in the height of such a promise as that from which John F. Kennedy was violently snatched last week.

Indeed, he had marched beyond mere promise. He stood in the most crucial arena of fulfilment which modern society offers to anyone of the human race. He was a man of large gifts with large opportunities of using them. His office laid upon him many an hour of small routine. But there was nothing small in the issues which he transacted. Because he stood in the highest place he commanded the broadest view of the human condition which anyone can hope to attain. To the challenge of this fortune he responded with an eager intellectual zest. He knew the price of failure as well as the incomparable reward of success. "Never have the nations of the world had so much to lose or so much to gain" he told the United Nations. "Together we shall save our planet or together we shall perish in its flames."

You will notice in his speeches a frequent recourse to such formulations as these. The theme is that of choice between sharp alternatives, an acute contast between potentialities of salvation and threats of doom. This is the first generation in which such choices have been confronted. Absolute destruction and

125

unlimited abundance are two possibilities neither of which has ever existed before. It happens that in our time they exist together. And each of them has its origin in the vast penetration of nature achieved by the evolving scientific intelligence of our times. Modern statesmanship stands at the point where great peril and great opportunity intersect. For the first time the subject of history is not a nation or a continent but the planet Earth itself.

John F. Kennedy marched towards this crushing burden because he wanted to be there. My memory of his senatorial days is of a restless energy constantly seeking broader fields of action. There was an unspoken assumption that he owed his nation a service commensurate with the gifts by which he had been endowed. And in our days the range and complexity of affairs demand a wide volume of knowledge. He was voracious in the quest for intellectual experience, a fluent speaker and—what is much more rare—a tense listener. Having equipped himself with every Presidential attribute which can be acquired beyond the gift of nature he struggled to his goal. He reached it three years ago this month.

He was young, of course, but yet ten years older than the 33-year-old Thomas Jefferson who drafted the Declaration of Independence and within one year of the 44-year-old George Washington who took office one hundred seventy-two years before. He belongs in historic terms to this company of men for whom the Presidency was not the crown to be worn in twilight but the legacy of men whose future was longer than their past. These were men who had a zest for life, who connected spiritual belief to political action, who sought the broadest possible personal development. For man's natural rights are not limited to the political rights alone. His natural rights have something to do with his place in the world and the stretching power of his spirit and talent. The biographer of Kennedy's election campaign, T. White, defined his essential conviction in terms of a belief that a man can change history and need not merely be changed by it.

Henceforward, the story is of what he did and how he did it.

It is easier to recount his actual deeds than it is to grasp and convey the style of his progress. But the story of what he did is impressive enough. In the domestic scene he pursued the cause of social progress without undue preoccupation with theory. If he valued the professors of economics it was because he wanted their intelligence, not because he was interested in their scientific generalisations. His philosophy, which was complex in other fields, did not go beyond the simple truths here. "If a free society cannot help the many who are poor, it cannot save the few who are rich." The legislative proposals of these three years deal with the very old and the very young, with social peace and educational vigour, with the utmost use of federal power in the pursuit of a just society in a land which, as Prof. Myrdal's recent book has proved, still has unconquered fields to traverse before the slogan of an affluent society becomes fully true.

Beyond economic justice lies social equality. Here there is a direct link between the central problem of American society and the driving force of international life. It is inconceivable that thirty African nations can enter the community of sovereign states without any consequent effect on minority groups seeking equal rights within a society. A statesman who promotes the liberation of subject nations abroad cannot fail to combat the relics of old prejudice and discrimination within his gate. Kennedy's ardent pursuit of national freedom in Africa and Asia, his expanded vision of foreign aid, his Peace Corps which revived the volunteer urge within a rich society threatened by the domination of private satisfactions—all these were bound to lead him back to the heritage of the great predecessor who on another dark Friday ninety-eight years ago laid his life upon the altar of freedom. In the struggle for free societies and the equal rights of men Lincoln and Kennedy are of a common lineage.

But what do economic justice or social equality mean without peace? Here, after all, is the crucial test. From his first contact with other nations, whether in concert or in conflict, he revealed the outlines of a new diplomatic talent. Here an American President moves on rocky ground. He deals with forces

127

which lie beyond his sovereign power. Adversaries are difficult, allies almost impossible. Small nations need a more sensitive touch than great powers. The world does not revolve around Washington and Moscow alone. The Communist and still more the non-Communist world, present a pattern of pluralism, diversity, variety, evolution, growth. No two international problems are alike. And all these issues tend to erupt in overlapping phases within a turmoil of constant change. The scene passes from Cuba to Laos, from Berlin to Vietnam, from Yemen to Cambodia. But it is never a tranquil scene. The only unchanging fact in history is the fact of change.

Amidst such dangers there is little hope in generalised attitudes, still less in slogans. To be always pliable is only slightly more ridiculous than to be always firm. The essence of the problem is to know when to evince flexibility and when to put the barriers firmly into place. It is not a science or a grammar to be learned by repetition. It partakes more of art than of science. It is a product of a creative intuition rather than of a mechanical rule of thumb. It is an exquisite application of judgment. Above all, it is very important not to be wrong. Here, and here alone, a major error is beyond repair or consolation. What is called the loneliness of the Presidency is, in large measure, the consequence of its international responsibility. Counsel may be shared. Responsibility is unsharable. This distinguishes the Presidency from the Cabinet system and creates the poignant solitude which a President inhabits from his first minute of office to his last.

That John Kennedy possessed this special intuition is proved by two episodes. One is the Cuban crisis when he stared the most fearful possibility in the face. That night he must have undergone an experience quite different in degree or quality from what anyone else, except his two predecessors, can ever have understood. Another episode on the converse side of the coin was the breakthrough, if such it proves to be, on the nuclear tests. In each case different qualities were summoned to action. I do not underestimate the potentiality of the Alliance for Progress or the rich promise of European Union if I say that these two inter-bloc crises were Kennedy's main testing grounds.

It is, of course, impossible for any political leader to be always right and somewhat difficult ever to be right at all. Carl Sandburg, Lincoln's biographer, has reflected wisely on this. "If he opens any door of policy, he is sure to hear it should be opened wider; or that it should be closed entirely; or that there should be a new door; or a return to the door that was there before; or that the original intention of the Founding Fathers was that a window is better than a door anyhow."

I believe that posterity will say of John F. Kennedy that he knew when to open the door and when to keep it shut. If we are wrong in this there will be no posterity to declare the error.

It is grievous to reflect on the loss of such a union of experience and authority in the service of great decisions.

So much for what John Kennedy managed to perform in three short years that have become an epoch. The bare account grossly underestimates the scope of the transformation which he wrought. To grasp this transformation we must invoke the image and the style which he conveyed to statecraft. It was a fresh, new wind born of the twentieth century. (He was the first leader of a great Power to have been born in the twentieth century.) This is the generation of men who were born in one war, who have survived a second, and whose main energies have since been devoted to the avoidance of a third. It is a generation whose political perils and technological environment might well have reduced to cold, hard, icy habits of thought and action, were its asperities not softened by ancient truth and by humane compassion. Here lies the importance of Kennedy's role in bringing intellectual excellence into the service of statecraft. He knew that a statesman's stature now depended on the quality of the ideas in his mind, not on the number of telephones on his desk. He rebelled against the conventional belief that a gulf is drawn between those who act and those who think. The task today is to translate mediation and loftiness of purpose into deeds. However scarce truth may be, there is always a greater supply than demand. Statecraft must be impelled

129

by a sense of intellectual adventure. Without adventure civilization is in full decay. The elevation of art and science to the centre of a nation's life is not the least of the innovations of the Kennedy era. Another is the high value he set on incisiveness of expression. There are, after all, only two ways of governing man. One is through violence and tyranny, and it brooks no discussion. The other is through speech. The word *logos* meant both speech and reason with the Greeks. In Hebrew thought "prophecy" (*nebuah*) is fundamentally "expression." Pericles' speech contains the pronouncement "The man who can think and does not know how to express what he thinks is at the level of him who cannot think." The Kennedy Presidency is a triumphant exercise of the power of communication across a continent—and across the seas.

One of the domains in which this communication was free and vivid was in the dialogue between the United States and Israel. It is not only that he was Israel's friend. Such a definition underestimates the truth. He did not merely inherit a tradition from his predecessors. He strengthened and enlarged it into new directions. These matters are still too fresh for public treatment. When the American-Israel dialogue of these three years is fully examined it will be found to have rested in his mind on a deep historical insight into our people's ancient splendour, its recent martyrdom, its modern renewal, its present danger and its future hope. From his ancestral Ireland and his native Massachusetts he had learned something about the cultural fertility of small communities. He knew that beyond the realm of quantity and matter there lay the more enduring domain of quality and spirit. In these terms Israel's smallness is a relative and even a misleading concept. Because he grasped our history intellectually he could grasp it spiritually. He felt himself and his countrymen to be bound by a commitment to Israel's security and progress. I have a feeling that he saw this not as a burden, but as a grace.

There are other chapters in this story for which the scope of words is still too narrow. The horrifying split-second transition from youthful vigor to a great and awful silence, the pain of widowhood and orphanhood both enhanced and assuaged by public scrutiny, the question mark which will eternally hover over what might have been. "The whole earth" wrote the Greek historian "is the sepulchre of famous men; and their story is graven not only on stone over their native earth, but lives on far away, without visible symbol, woven into the stuff of other men's lives."

I believe that our lives have something in them which is of the fabric of these past three years. Rarely has a statesman had a more universal sepulchre in distant lands. Yesterday the rocking-chair was taken out of the White House. The Kennedy era passes from the realm of visible symbols into that of historic memory. There will, of course, be other eras of zest and vitality, when men feel that it is morning and that it is good to be alive. This, however, belongs to the future. In the meantime let us be frank with each other. The world is darker than it was a week ago.

Murray Kempton,
The Spectator, London

A certain indifference, preferably even a certain laziness seems to have been essential to the Kennedy tone. Without that, mere piety works dreadful damage to taste and comprehension; the written word being sacred can only be read as literal and culture, being sacred, has a particular responsibility to be respectable. Mr. Kennedy's style depended on that sense of proportion only possible to a man who has limited his pride to those parts of himself he judges important enough to be proud about.

I, as an instance, bear the guilt of having written, while struggling to fix him in my mind, a number of tasteless and, what is less excusable, some quite careless things to Mr. Kennedy's detraction before he was elected. If he had a fault, it was the expense of too much time on newspapers; and he read everything even the humblest of us wrote. Yet, a few days after what even I had to concede was a dreadful excess and one which, by mere bad taste, had achieved such notoriety that Mr. Kennedy could not have escaped it, I encountered him and was greeted with entire cordiality. He was, to be sure, an immensely polite man; but he was certainly too spirited to let pass unrebuked any hit at a point of real personal pride. Whatever my excesses, I had never—at a guess—said that he would lie or leave a wounded man under enemy gunfire or that, whatever other defect my inflamed fancy might invent, he was not an entirely charming man. He had the sense to know that charm is an absolute virtue. He seems to have read *J.F.K., The Man and the Myth*, though it seemed a protracted exercise in spite, with complete equanimity about its judgment of himself. Its author, we can see now, had been sustained in his labors by the mere sight of a man who offended him by being so graceful, so dashing and so gallant. That animus has, of course, been decently interred after Dallas, but when it and he were alive, Mr. Kennedy was confronting an enemy aroused not *in spite of* but almost *because* of his charm, an enemy indeed who gave the most concentrated attention to the president's most attractive qualities under the delusion that they were defects. Mr. Kennedy then could hardly not have enjoyed reading someone who set down to his credit all these virtues even though it was someone with taste so distorted that he persisted in arraigning them as vices.

*Letters from four students
from Tananarive, Madagascar, to Mrs. Kennedy
and the children,
November 28th, 1963*

Tananarive, Thanksgiving Day, 1963

To: Mrs. Jacqueline Kennedy, Caroline and John
Through: His Excellency United States Ambassador in
    Madagascar
Through: The Head of American Cultural Center Tananarive

M adam:

Allow us to testify very respectfully that we feel greatly for
the unbelievable death of the President John F. Kennedy. We
know him especially through the movies we see every Thursday
at The American Cultural Center and through books we read
there.

Please, excuse us. We only write to assure you how much we
feel for you under this severe and sudden bereavement. Human
words are powerless to console you, for deep is your despair and
great is your grief.

Kindly then remember God's Words: "Leave thy fatherless
children, I will preserve them alive, and let thy widows trust in
Me", (Jer. 49 1-11) "For I know the thoughts that I think toward you, saith The Lord, thoughts of peace, and not of evil, to
give you an expected end." (Jer. 29/11).

You will find, Madam, we are sure, in your love for your children, the strength to be comforted. They will be the tender and
living image of your husband and will bring you the sweetest
and the most efficacious consolations. The interest and the happiness of your little ones require that you should keep up your
spirits.

Moreover, believe us, your husband, the object of your grief
and that of all nations, is not dead. He lives, by the great quality

of his heart and mind, in a better world. No! His memory cannot perish.

THE PRESIDENT JOHN F. KENNEDY IS IMMORTAL.

We end by Mr. Lutteroth's oration at the time of Jean Frédéric Oberlin's funeral: "Nous avons raconté ce qui s'est passé sur la terre, mais qui de nous, après avoir ou le cercueil descendre dans la fosse, n' a pas levé les yeux dans le sentiment de ce qui se passe au ciel. Si les hommes pleurent aujourd'hui, il y a de la joie parmi les anges; si le temps a perdu un juste, l'éternité a gagné un saint."

Our parents unite with us to pray to God to give you strength necessary to hold up with resignation under the blow that Providence has inflicted you.

MAY GOD HAVE CAROLINE AND JOHN IN HIS HOLY KEEPING!

Believe us, Madam, to remain,

Yours devotedly,

Percy Myriam Rasoazanamialy, 16 years
2nd. form—Lycée Jules Ferry
Radilimanantsoa-Raveloherifera Jedidias, 14 years
3rd. form—Lycée Galliéni
Jeliarizel Christophin Sederavololomasoandro, 12 years
4th form—Lycée Galliéni
Jocelyn Christian Rakotomahandry, 11 years
6th form—Lycée Galliéni

Karan Singh,
Sadar-i-Riyasat of Jammu and Kashmir,
Times of India, Bombay,
December 1st, 1963

I had never met him, but his dynamic presence came through even from seeing his photographs and reading his speeches—the boyish shock of hair, the friendly grin, the eyes youthful but mature, the determined chin, the whole personality keyed to action and achievement.

I recall vividly the night he was elected. For various reasons I, along with many thousands of other Indians, was emotionally deeply committed to his victory. He seemed to enshrine a promise for a brighter future, for a liberal, dynamic and creative policy which would help us all create a better world. He was not very much younger than his opponent, but somehow I felt he was the personification of youthful maturity. He was fourteen years older than I, but though I had never met him I felt for him an affinity difficult to explain but clearly experienced.

On the night of the presidential election I happened to be in a suite at Rashtrapati Bhavan where I was attending the annual Governors' conference. I stayed glued to the radio almost throughout the night in a state of high excitement. There was no conclusive news that night, but the trend was hopeful and I finally slept for a couple of hours fairly sanguine about his victory. The next morning we were in the midst of the conference when a messenger came in bearing a chit on a silver tray which he handed to the Prime Minister. He read it and then interrupted the proceedings with the remark: "Kennedy has won the election." It took all my power of self-control to prevent myself jumping up and dancing round the table. The Prime Minister was also visibly pleased.

And then since his election I followed his movements and statements with care—not merely because he was the head of the most powerful nation in the world but because for me he symbolised the new post-war leadership upon whose shoulders must inevitably rest the destiny of the human race. In my own country almost all the people who matter in politics are more than twice my age, and so in Kennedy I felt there was a spirit more kindred.

I had occasion to meet his gracious wife when she visited India last year. And there were other features in Kennedy's life which drew me to him as, in a way, they paralleled my own experience—his aristocratic background but democratic career; his family life; the fact that he spent many months in bed due to a physical disability. And so when the news of his assassination broke, a thrill of sorrow shot through me, an incredulous shock which was felt throughout the world. My first reaction was one of despair and bewilderment. There must be something radically wrong with the design of this world if its most promising and dynamic life could be snuffed out by the hand of a misguided—or perhaps carefully guided—fanatic.

But on further thought, when I weighed the event in the context of certain deeply-held convictions, the despair vanished and the pain became bearable. I believe that there is a certain pattern and power that governs human destiny, and that this death—epic as it is in its tragic dimensions—is not, cannot be, in vain. Indeed, some deeper purpose must be served by the sacrifice—the consummation for example of the heroic battle of the American Negro for full democratic rights and dignity. What is more, I believe that the human soul is immortal and indestructable, and that the soul of John Fitzgerald Kennedy has not perished along with his body.

And then there was a certain heroic dignity in the manner of his going—no prolonged illness, no tortured screams of pain and fear. At one moment he was there in the plenitude of his powers—waving to the joyous crowd that thronged to see him. The next moment, his destiny fulfilled, he fell. Is that not the truest destiny of man—the glorious creativity of life, the unutterable mystery of death?

Editorial,
Teen Talk, West Kinney Jr. High School,
Newark, New Jersey

He was a friend . . . our hope . . . a member of the family. He was like a father . . . or a bigger brother . . ."

Such were the words and thoughts of bewilderment, confusion and fright cried out by West Kinney Jr. High students on that black Friday afternoon when we first learned of the assassination of President John Fitzgerald Kennedy.

It was like being struck and slapped at the same time! He is not dead! He can't be! This is a horrible, horrible dream and I want to wake up. But no one at West Kinney, in Newark, in America or most of the world could sleep or pass off the dreadful Dallas death of young John F. Kennedy.

Who would want to kill our President?

America and the world had lost a great and gifted leader. But Negroes had lost their greatest Friend since Abraham Lincoln.

Mr. Kennedy was the first President most of us remembered with our own eyes and hearts. We heard and read of Lincoln and FDR but we looked at, loved and often listened to Mr. Kennedy.

140

He was a warm, personal and live experience in our daily lives. He was the first leader of this era who really seemed to care about us . . . about what we thought . . . about how we felt . . . about where we wanted to belong.

He inspired us with his confidence. He dared us to be hopeful because he was hopeful. He was like Jackie Robinson and Jimmy Brown. A real champion.

Perhaps we are not old enough to completely understand political differences between parties and men. But we did know that this man was great.

When we heard the news we were too shocked to believe it. We remembered that we hadn't wanted to believe the death of Medgar Evers or the Birmingham children's murder either. But we had to. And so we face this tragic period with the thought that we have lost a friend, but we were lucky to have had him for three years.

America will continue under President Johnson's leadership, and we will live to do our share in making democracy work.

Sander Vanocur,
NBC Television,
November 30th, 1963

A part of each of us was buried Monday.

We are, as a people, the sum of those who went before us, lived and died, and put their mark upon what we are and what we must become.

If the President was the living symbol of a people—of our past, our present and our future—then a part of each of us died with him and a part of each of us was buried Monday.

If we had reposed in this good man, now departed, our hopes, our dreams, our fears and the love and hate we bear each other, then a part of each of us died with him.

But if he lives in our memories, and if his spirit casts light upon the darkness—as the flame on his grave illuminates a small plot of our hallowed earth—then life has sprung from that which is dead, and that part of each of us which was buried Monday may live again.

Let those who would search for symbolism in these words—search not. There is none. We do not deify John Fitzgerald Kennedy. We remember him. If it is for the dead to inspire the living, it is for the living to honor the dead. For us, there is nothing more but to say—Thank you, Mister President—and —Farewell.

142

Karl E. Meyer,
New Statesman, November 29th, 1963

He came in with a snowstorm, and the setting was flawlessly right on Inauguration Day, 20 January 1961. There was no premonition of tragedy, but rather a sense of rebirth in a capital mantled in beauty as the oldest President yielded power to the youngest man ever elected Chief Executive of the United States. More than a change of administrations, it was a change of generations, a change of outlook—and most immediately apparent, a change of style. When John Fitzgerald Kennedy was sworn in, he appeared to fulfil Robert Frost's augury that an age of poetry and power was commencing in Washington. But the poetry is now hushed, and the promise of power wisely used is now an unfinished chapter in a volume entitled, "Let Us Begin. . ." None of us suspected that in retrospect the Inaugural snow would seem as a shroud.

It is too early to fix Mr. Kennedy's place in history because so much of what he initiated was left for others to complete. But two of his achievements seem likely to take root. He was not a man given to easy commitments, but before his death he embarked on two major ventures—for the first time in this century, he placed the power and might of his office behind a dispossessed race whose second-class status demeaned all citizens; at the same time, he took the world to the precipice of a war but followed his unexampled personal triumph by deeds intended to eliminate the risk of a holocaust through madness or miscalculation. The special pathos of his death is that he seemed on the verge of broadening his commitment.

Something else, however, is irretrievably lost—the brilliance of his presence, the glow of his style. To Americans like myself who were near to his age, he renewed our pride in our country and gave a dignity to the political calling. If we fretted at his failures and reproached him for his excessive caution, it was because he seemed more a brother than father, and because we judged him in terms of his capacity for greater things. His unfailing wit, which he could turn on himself, his literacy, his physical grace and his sense of history were part of a harmonious whole. By virtue of television, and his superb performance at press conferences, he became in life an intensely personal figure to millions; in death he leaves a mournful void.

A prodigious reader, he cherished not only learning, but the learned. His ideal of government seemed to be half academy, half precinct-headquarters. He opened the White House to anybody who could impart a ferment and his good humour as a host was legend. His favourite biography was Lord David Cecil's *Melbourne*, and the choice tells a good deal about the strengths and weaknesses of his self-definition. Like the urbane Whigs of Melbourne's age, he blended a studied detachment, broad if conventional interest in the arts, moderate liberalism, family pride and belief in reason. It is savage irony that this child of the Enlightenment was cut down by the very fanaticism that he sought to contain. The cause for which he stood remains in doubt, and the last page of his biography must be written with what Virgil called the tears of things.

Editorial,
The Virginian-Pilot, Norfolk,
November 26th, 1963

In scarlet and blue and green and purple, three by three the sovereigns rode, with plumed helmets, gold braid, crimson sashes and jeweled orders flashing in the sun. After them came five heirs apparent, 40 more imperial or royal highnesses, seven queens and a scattering of special ambassadors from uncrowned countries. Together they represented 70 nations in the greatest assemblage of royalty and rank ever gathered in one place, and of its kind, the last."

Barbara Tuchman, *The Guns of August*

The kings who followed a black riderless horse on May 20, 1910, when Britain buried King Edward VII and those who followed another black riderless horse when President John Fitzgerald Kennedy was buried yesterday alike mourned men who were central to their time.

After the death of Edward VII there were but a few years left to the age of comfort and established order to which historians have given his name, and much of the royalty represented in his funeral procession was snuffed out in the upheaval.

In 1914, when the guns of August began to roar, Viscount Grey stood by his study window and said to a visitor, "The lamps are going out all over Europe; we shall not see them lit again in our lifetime." When the lamps went out, the hopes of men for a world at peace dimmed and flickered, not to be revived until a war had been fought "to make the world safe for democracy," and another and greater had to be fought over the embers of the first, and a "police action" fought in Korea, and a host of lesser wars.

The great came from all over the world yesterday to pay their respects to the man who had begun to light the lamps in our time.

145

A dozen members of reigning royal families, 18 presidents, 35 foreign and defense ministers, representing 53 nations, they came to mourn the man who embodied the hope of a peaceful tomorrow for the whole world.

Far more than Americans realize, the 46-year-old President with the boyish good looks, the father of two young children, the man with the quick mind and ready wisecrack, represented freedom and generosity and man's good will to man for the entire Free World and for those who aspired to freedom in the lands of the unfree.

To the Berliners who lit candles in thousands of windows in honor of the man who had only recently told them, *Ich bin ein Berliner;* to the Africans and the British and the Irish; to the millions who felt his loss as a personal stab and sought to express their sympathy in some way, he was the good man who tried to bridle the forces of unlimited destruction and find a path to the sunny uplands.

It was to the generation who talk of World War II as "their" war, and to those younger yet who hope to be spared "their" war, that Mr. Kennedy particularly seemed to speak. It is their idealism and intelligence that he mustered, and they grieve for his brave young widow with special understanding.

In the few months between the Cuban confrontation and the assassination of the President so senselessly last Friday, there seemed to be the beginnings of the chance of reaching some understanding, the chance of lighting lamps for tomorrow. That hope must not be buried with the President.

Let us look to the first few lamps that John Kennedy lit throughout the world.

146

Dear Caroline'

I am sorry your Daddy has died. I have a very nice Daddy That I will share with you and your broTher.

I am your friend'

Lisa Downes.

W hy have we wept?
Why do the Americas have their eyes filled with tears and regard the death of a man as an irreparable loss?

Why does underdeveloped, romantic, anxious, gentlemanly
and virile Latin America suffer?

What is the reason for our tears? Do not great men who have
devoted their lives to the welfare of mankind die every day?
Aren't they constantly being born, developing and fading
away?

Why do we all feel such a deep and sincere sorrow for the
tragic, brutal, sudden loss of President Kennedy?

If we can find out the reason for this continent-wide grief
and if we can determine why Spanish America bleeds as though
we ourselves were wounded by the fatal bullet that ended the
life of President Kennedy, we will be on the threshold of a true
policy of co-existence, of unity, of faith and of Pan-American
understanding long sought by men, who sometimes walked in
the dark, often made mistakes, and who failed to find that
hidden motive which is the reason for our tears today.

We do not believe we are mistaken if we assume that, at least
partially, the motive is the coincidence of similar fundamental
values shared by Latin Americans and President Kennedy.
Thus his death has brought upon us shattering pain today.

We admire many men, we respect a lot of them and the news
of their death would move us. But with Kennedy the Latin
American reaction has been different. It has been much more
human and more affectionate. We all feel that he who has died
is not only a statesman, or a great leader, but also a human
being; a truly great man who had the same sweet and warm
feeling for his home that we Latin Americans have; a man who

149

had in his hands the staggering responsibility of the future of the world, yet with those same hands he caressed his children. A young man, full of energy and vitality, who faced the most far-reaching problems of world politics with the same tenacity and sagacity as he would fighting for racial integration of his nation, feeling, as we do, that all people should enjoy equal rights regardless of race or color. A man who professed our own faith, a devout Catholic, who shared our belief in the moral order of the universe. A millionaire who would rebel at the sight of our legions of hungry men, who like us was concerned over the lack of housing for our people, who would suffer because in tropical America illiteracy was the rule, and who would dream, along with all of us, of a future of free men, free from hunger, from ignorance, and from sickness. A man who loved his wife, who loved democracy and who made us realize that his heart sheltered such love. President Kennedy was a man, finally, such as we Latin Americans believe men should be. The United States had another President who has always been a source of inspiration for all Latin Americans. He died, like Kennedy, on a Friday under the impact of an evil bullet, and like Kennedy he dreamed of equality among white and colored men. This man is venerated today in Latin America as much as, or even more than he is in the United States for what he did as a statesman and for what he stood for as a man. He came from a humble home, a very poor and extraordinarily unstable home. His life, as well as his death, is compared today with that of Kennedy who came from a distinguished and wealthy background. It is on the human coincidence, on the coincidence of views, on the sharing of values which existed between Abraham Lincoln and John F. Kennedy that the origin of our tears lies, as well as the secret for a harmonious and candid policy between Latin America and the United States, a Nation capable of producing a Lincoln from its lowest strata, and a Kennedy from its highest strata.

There are no nationalities nor races in the ideal world of values. When we all realized that Kennedy was with us on earth, when we learned that like us he worshipped God, loved his children, had concern for his fellowmen, fought for peace, desired physical and spiritual well-being for all mankind, reacted the same way we do, with our own anxieties and burdens, we held him as ours, and it is as ours that we have lost him.

We believe it is important that Latin Americans and North Americans should ask themselves: Why have we wept in Latin America? Why the tears? The future of a Continent may well depend on the answers to these questions.

Andrew Sinclair,
The Sunday Telegraph, London,
November 24th, 1963

Today, Harvard weeps for her favourite son. John F. Kennedy was a Harvard man. No one could forget him. Harvard was in his mind, his dress, his tongue. He knew he was meant to rule, with courage and integrity. Although he was rich, he was taught that his duty was to serve the poor.

Harvard and Massachusetts used to be a power in the American Government. For more than a century, they had lost that power. John F. Kennedy put Harvard back in the White House. Not since Woodrow Wilson had such an educated man been President.

But if Kennedy did much for Harvard, Harvard had done much for him. Once it had been a centre of the Abolitionists, who had helped to free the Negro slaves. Now it was a Harvard man who was trying to push through the greatest freedom for the Negro in a hundred years.

Kennedy had been destined for academics. Until the death of his elder brother, he had chosen the library rather than the hustings. Even in politics, he remained a Harvard man. When in the Senate, he was elected as a member of the Harvard governing body by the largest vote of graduates up to that time.

As President, he did not forget Harvard. His advisers were often drawn from Harvard and the Massachusetts Institute of Technology. And he could be faithful enough, while occupying the most powerful place on earth, to drop in on a Harvard football game only a month ago. Land by the Charles River has already been set aside to build a library to house the Kennedy papers.

If John F. Kennedy did not forget Harvard, Harvard did not forget him. When he was shot, work stopped. No one spoke. All listened to the wireless.

No one spoke in the Yard or in Harvard Square. Occasionally, to a stranger or a driver, a voice said, "Have you heard?" Or simply, "He's dead." In Widener Library, a girl wept with hysteria.

Outside, on the grass, the grey squirrels were the only things that stirred. The students stood still, alone, in groups. The air was dazed. There was a silence. No one could move or speak. The flags fell to half-mast.

The bells in Memorial Church began to toll. One student hit a tree with his fist. Again and again, he hit the tree. An unknown man lay on the grass on his stomach. He was crying.

Harvard's President, Nathan M. Pusey, said that John F. Kennedy, "was one who made wise and effective use of the world of learning and we mourn him as a friend. His only ambition was to serve his country and he gave his life for it."

A line of students stood by the newspaper stand in the Square. No one could believe the news. "Did you hear?" "Yes." "Is it true?" "Yes." And they waited for the newspapers to say in print what they feared to believe in themselves.

Harvard has lost more than an honorary Doctor of Laws, who was given his degree with the inscription, "brave officer, able Senator, Son of Harvard; loyal to party, he remained steadfast to principle."

Lost is an intellectual in the White House, a good historian, a man who believed in learning and in compromise for peace and in the values of the mind.

Government must go on. Harvard must go on. She has made Presidents before and will make them again. If there are tears and silence now, they are to mourn a great man, who would have laughed at the child in Harvard Yard who asked *if* America would get another President.

Mary McGrory,
Washington Star,
November 23rd, 1963

He brought gaiety, glamor and grace to the American political scene in a measure never known before. That lightsome tread, that debonair touch, that shock of chestnut hair, that beguiling grin, that shattering understatement—these are what we shall remember.

He walked like a prince and he talked like a scholar. His humor brightened the life of the Republic. While striving for his great office, he had often concealed his amusement at the incongruities of life, lest he be thought not only youthful but frivolous as well. When safely ensconced, he saw no reason to hide his wit. It glinted at every press conference. It informed his private utterance. Shown his latest nephew in August, he commented, "He looks like a fine baby—we'll know more later."

One day he strolled onto the porch outside his office and found an old friend admiring the garden. The lawn was a source of unreasoning pride and constant concern to him; the flowers, while he was uncertain of their names, pleased him. He indicated the tangle of petunias and ageratum and said dryly, "This may go down as the real achievement of this administration."

His public statements were always temperate, always measured. He derided his enemies—he teased his friends. He could be grave, but not for long.

When the ugliness of yesterday has been forgotten, we shall remember him, smiling.

E. B. White,
The New Yorker,
November 30th, 1963

When we think of him, he is without a hat, standing in the wind and the weather. He was impatient of topcoats and hats, preferring to be exposed, and he was young enough and tough enough to confront and to enjoy the cold and the wind of these times, whether the winds of nature or the winds of political circumstance and national danger. He died of exposure, but in a way that he would have settled for—in the line of duty, and with his friends and enemies all around, supporting him and shooting at him. It can be said of him, as of few men in a like position, that he did not fear the weather, and did not trim his sails, but instead challenged the wind itself, to improve its direction and to cause it to blow more softly and more kindly over the world and its people.

155

Courage is the virtue that President Kennedy most admired. He sought out those people who had demonstrated in some way, whether it was on a battlefield, or a baseball diamond, in a speech, or fighting for a cause, that they had courage, that they would stand up, that they could be counted on. . . .

As Andrew Jackson said, "One man with courage makes a majority." That is the effect President Kennedy had on others.

President Kennedy would have been 47 in May of 1964. At least one half of the days that he spent on this earth were days of intense physical pain. He had diphtheria when he was very young and serious back trouble when he was older. In between, he had almost every other conceivable ailment. When we were growing up together, we used to laugh about the great risk a mosquito took in biting Jack Kennedy—with some of his blood the mosquito was almost sure to die. He was in Chelsea Naval Hospital for an extended period of time after the war, had a major and painful operation on his back in 1954, campaigned on crutches in 1958. In 1951, on a trip we took around the world, he became ill. We flew to the military hospital in Okinawa and he had a temperature of over 106 degrees. They didn't think he would live.

But during all this time, I never heard him complain. I never heard him say anything which would indicate that he felt that God had dealt with him unjustly. Those who knew him well would know he was suffering only because his face was a little whiter, the lines around his eyes were a little deeper, his words a little sharper. Those who did not know him well detected nothing.

He didn't complain about his problem so why should I complain about mine—that is how one always felt.

When he battled against illness, when he fought in the war, when he ran for the Senate, when he stood up against powerful interests in Massachusetts to fight for the St. Lawrence Seaway, when he fought for a labor reform act in 1959, when he entered the West Virginia primary in 1960, when he debated Lyndon Johnson at the Democratic Convention in Los Angeles with no preparation, when he took the blame completely on himself for the failure at the Bay of Pigs, when he fought the steel companies, when he stood up at Berlin in 1961 and then again in 1962 for the freedom of that city, when he forced the withdrawal of the Soviet missiles from Cuba, when he spoke and fought for equal rights for all our citizens, and hundreds of other things both big and small, he was reflecting what is the best in the human being.

He was demonstrating conviction, courage, a desire to help others who needed help, and true and genuine love for his country.

Because of his efforts, the mentally retarded and the mentally ill will have a better chance, the young a greater opportunity to be educated and live with dignity and self-respect, the ill to be cared for, the world to live in peace.

President Kennedy had only a thousand days in the White House instead of 3,000 days, yet so much was accomplished. Still so much needs to be done.

President Kennedy was fond of quoting Dante that "the hottest places in Hell are reserved for those who, in a time of great moral crisis, maintain their neutrality."

If there is a lesson from the life of John Kennedy and from his death, it is that in this world of ours none of us can afford to be lookers-on, the critics standing on the sidelines.

Thomas Carlyle wrote: "The courage we desire and prize is not the courage to die decently but to live manfully."

On the morning of his death, President Kennedy called former Vice-President John Nance Garner to pay his respects. It was Mr. Garner's 95th birthday. When Mr. Garner first came to Washington, the total Federal budget was less than 500 million dollars. President Kennedy was administering a budget of just under 100 billion dollars.

President Kennedy's grandmother was living in Boston when he was assassinated. She was also alive the year President Lincoln was shot. We are a young country. We are growing and expanding until it appears that this planet will no longer contain us. We have problems now that people fifty, even ten years ago, would not have dreamed would have to be faced.

The energies and talents of all of us are needed to meet the challenges, the internal ones of our cities, our farms, ourselves; to be successful in the fight for freedom around the globe; in the battles against illiteracy, hunger and disease. Pleasantries, self-satisfied mediocrity will serve us badly. We need the best of many—not of just a few. We must strive for excellence.

Lord Tweedsmuir, one of the President's favorite authors, wrote in his autobiography: "Public life is the crown of a career, and to young men it is the worthiest ambition. Politics is still the greatest and most honorable adventure."

It has been fashionable in many places to look down on politics, on those in Government. President Kennedy, I think, changed that and altered the public conception of Government. He certainly did for those who participated. But, however we feel about politics, the arena of Government is where the decisions will be made affecting not only all our destinies, but the future of our children born and unborn.

At the time of the Cuban missile crisis last year, we discussed the possibility of war, a nuclear exchange, and being killed—the latter at that time seemed so unimportant, almost frivolous. The one matter which really was of concern to him and truly had meaning and made that time much more fearful than it would otherwise have been, was the specter of death of the children of this country and around the world—the young people who had no part and knew nothing of the confrontation, but whose lives would be snuffed out like everyone else's. They would never have been given a chance to make a decision, to vote in an election, to run for office, to lead a revolution, to determine their own destinies.

158

We, our generation, had. And the great tragedy was that if we erred, it was that we erred not just for ourselves, our futures, our homes, our country, but for the lives, futures, homes and countries of those who never had been given an opportunity to play a role, to vote "aye" or "nay," to make themselves felt.

Bonar Law said: "There is no such thing as inevitable war. If war comes it will be from failure of human wisdom."

It is true. It is human wisdom that is needed not just on our side, but on all sides. I might add that if wisdom had not been demonstrated by the American President and also by Premier Khrushchev, then the world as we know it would have been destroyed.

But there will be future Cubas. There will be future crises. We have the problems of the hungry, the neglected, the poor and the downtrodden. They must receive more help. And just as solutions had to be found in October of 1962, answers must be found for these other problems that still face us. So that wisdom is needed still.

John Quincy Adams, Daniel Webster, Sam Houston, Thomas Hart Benton, Edmund G. Ross, Lucius Quintus Cincinnatus Lamar, George Norris, Robert Taft imparted a heritage to us. They came, they left their mark, and this country was not the same because these men had lived. How much the good of what they did and deeded to us was cherished, nurtured and encouraged, by so much the country and all of us gained.

And so it is also for John F. Kennedy. Like the lives of these others, his life had an import, meant something to the country while he was alive. More significant, however, is what we do with what is left, with what has been started. It was his conviction that the definition of citizenship in a democracy is participation in Government and that, as Francis Bacon wrote, it is "left only to God and to the angels to be lookers-on." It was his conviction that a democracy with this effort by its people must and can face its problems, that it must show patience, restraint, compassion, as well as wisdom and strength and courage in the struggle for solutions which are very rarely easy to find.

It was his conviction that we should do so successfully because the courage of those who went before us in this land exists in the present generation of Americans.

"We dare not forget today that we are the heirs of that first revolution. Let the word go forth from this time and place, to friend and foe alike, that the torch has been passed to a new generation of Americans—born in this century, tempered by war, disciplined by a hard and bitter peace, proud of our ancient heritage—and unwilling to witness or permit the slow undoing of those human rights to which this nation has always been committed, and to which we are committed today at home and around the world." . . .

What happens to the country, to the world, depends on what we do with what others have left us.

162